PROPERTY OF
DR. PARKER T. OBORN

CREATING AN ABUSE-FREE RELATIONSHIP

A Manual For Recovering Self and Intimacy

AF544911

Parker –
In sharing the beauty
of a gorgeous day –
May such natural joys
continue always for you,
Carolyn McGinnis
May 5, 2000

CREATING AN ABUSE-FREE RELATIONSHIP

A Manual For Recovering Self and Intimacy

CAROLYN S. McGINNIS, PH.D.

For use by therapists, support groups, domestic violence shelters, and individuals on a path of healing.

HEARTSFIRE BOOKS

© 1999
Carolyn S. McGinnis, Ph.D.
All Rights Reserved

All rights reserved. No part of this book may be reproduced or transmitted in any form or by any means, electronic or mechanical, including information storage and retrieval systems, without permission in writing from the publisher.

Library of Congress Cataloging-in-Publication Data

McGinnis, Carolyn Sue.
Creating an abuse free relationship: a manual for recovering self and intimacy/Carolyn S. McGinnis.—1st ed.
p. cm.
ISBN 1-889797-23-5 (pbk.): $16.95

1. Conjugal violence. 2. Wife abuse. 3. Husband abuse. 4. Psychological abuse. 5. Intimacy (Psychology) 6. Self-help techniques. I. Title.
MV6626.M415 1999 98–43215
158.2—dc21 CIP

Cover design by Cisneros Design
Text design and composition by John Cole GRAPHIC DESIGNER
Printed in Canada
Text is set in Palatino

First edition 1999
10 9 8 7 6 5 4 3 2 1

Heartsfire Books: 800.988.5170
500 N. Guadalupe Street, Suite G465
Santa Fe, New Mexico 87501 USA
Email: heartsfirebooks@heartsfirebooks.com
Visit us at http://www.heartsfirebooks.com

If you are unable to order this book from your local bookseller, you may order directly from the publisher. Quantity discounts for organizations are available.

More praise for Carolyn McGinnis' *CREATING AN ABUSE-FREE RELATIONSHIP:*

"What a gift it is to have a tool that is truly accessible to an individual in their unique personal journey toward well-being and whole relationships. This manual beautifully serves to soothe, explain, nourish, and enliven an individual's homeward journey to joy, healing, understanding, and wholeness."

Jean M. Keating, former Director, MCC Behavioral Care, Inc. (CIGNA, Inc.), Minneapolis, MN, and former Group Facilitator at CHRYSALIS, A Center For Women, Minneapolis, MN

"I gladly recommend Carolyn McGinnis' book. She frames the work on the relationship within the priority of safety, especially for the woman. It is important for both partners to have a support system beyond the relationship in order to work on these issues. These two factors are too often ignored or downplayed in relationship counseling, leading to the continuation of emotional and/or physical abuse."

Joseph Zdon, MSW, LISW, private practice, River Falls, WI; former Group Leader for Men's Domestic Violence Program, Wilder Foundation, St. Paul, MN

"I welcome Carolyn McGinnis' new self-help manual, ***CREATING AN ABUSE-FREE RELATIONSHIP: A Manual for Recovering Self and Intimacy***. This heartfelt guide book is insightful and thorough. It will be valuable both as a manual that someone can work through independently or as a resource for therapists working with clients who have traveled the painful road of abusive relationships. This book is another step in our collective struggle toward relationships that lead to healing and growth."

Ellen Franklin, Ph.D., Clinical Supervisor, Rape Crisis Center, Santa Fe, NM

"***CREATING AN ABUSE-FREE RELATIONSHIP: A Manual for Recovering Self and Intimacy*** provides a deeper level of healing intervention than most self-help books. It combines metaphysical concepts with more standard psychological ones and emphasizes the possibility for change even in those who have been on the abusing end."

Kate Piersanti, Berrett-Koehler Publishers and owner, Headland Productions

"Carolyn McGinnis has written a gentle guide to freedom and liberation for those who have been hurt by others. It is an invitation to begin a fruitful pilgrimage of self-realization and liberation."

Wayne Muller, author of *LEGACY OF THE HEART* (Simon and Schuster), and *HOW, THEN, SHALL WE LIVE?* (Bantam Books)

" A clearly written, thought-provoking guide to healing from an abusive past."

Aphrodite Matsakis, Ph.D., author of *TRUST AFTER TRAUMA: A Guide to Relationships for Surivivors* (New Harbinger Publications)

For those sufferers from trauma who,

in their healing,

make this a better world;

and for those who caused suffering and recovered.

CONTENTS

ACKNOWLEDGEMENTS

I am grateful to those who helped so much in forming this book: Linda Wing, who gave supportive editing early on; Kate Piersanti at Berrett-Koehler Publishing, who gave encouragement just in the nick of time; Sara Held for her superb editing skills as well as her level-headed comprehension of my task; and to Claude Saks for his vote of confidence. Foremost, I thank T.L.M., who almost always enthusiastically carried a huge part of the burden of rewrite after rewrite and deserves so much credit for making this dream come true.

I am especially appreciative of both clients and friends who have opened their hearts to me. Their trust in me, and my opportunity to help, has been my greatest satisfaction.

I have succeeded in my task if just some of the love, compassion, and inspiration of my mentor, Rakeich, comes through to the reader. This is a small part I do, and the book could not have been written without him.

CHAPTER ONE

PART ONE

INTRODUCTION

If you are currently experiencing abuse in a relationship, this book is written to help you extricate yourself, to lift yourself up and out of the abuse. If you have a history of abuse or failed relationships, this book is written to help you understand the misguided needs or expectations you bring to a relationship. And it is written to help you heal old wounds, set your goals, determine behaviors that meet these goals or not, and find health in a new, intimate partnership.

People struggle for power in their relationships, but when there is abuse, one person is dominating the other. Both participants may be abusive at the same time. Or both may change roles periodically. Domestic violence occurs for three reasons: the existence of human aggression, our culture's permissive attitudes towards violence, and the dynamics of intimate relationships. Moreover, though, the participants are out of heart. By this I mean that they are not connected to each other with open hearts, expressing qualities that come from the heart, like patience, kindness, and generosity.

If you are being physically intimidated, dominated, or abused, it is most likely, but not always the case, that you are a woman and the person exerting power over you is a man; but you may be a man who is being manipulated, cajoled, or humiliated. Whatever your situation, this book is written to help you. You will need to step into your own shoes, possess your own life, assert yourself. This book's focus will be on you alone, on you in a partnership, and on you and your partner as a couple. Underlying all of the suggested practices and reflections, and underlying the theme throughout, however, is a focus toward existing in heart with yourself and others.

Both partners in a relationship need and deserve help in changing. If you are being abused, in contrast to your partner, you might initially feel you have more to gain by seeking help because you are going to gain power over your own life. Your partner is preoccupied with controlling *you*, so he or she will experience loss when you are no longer able to be controlled. However, whichever role you are in, you will both gain power over your own lives and can join in a journey of equality, mutuality, and kindness.

It is absolutely incumbent upon our cultural and legal systems to require abusers to change. It is equally important that anyone being abused require, in his or her own heart, mind, and actions, that the abuse stop.

USER'S GUIDE TO THIS BOOK

This book is written to help you determine if domestic violence is occurring in your life and, if it is, how to change it. And it is written to help you if you have experienced abuse in the past and find it affecting your current relationships. This book will provide clear pictures of abuse by describing it in familiar behavioral terms. Inferences and practice suggestions will help you work from your own feelings and experiences to see the contrast between positive and negative interactions. There will be an educational focus combined with a motivational one, as this book is intended to help you see and set your goals on a better life for yourself.

We will work together to help you feel encouraged and energized, rather than experiencing the shame and pain you may currently feel in your life. We will deal openly and assertively with the fact of sexual and domestic violence, keeping in mind historical and cultural origins. This is a problem much broader than your individual situation. With this book, we call upon our cultural systems to make far-reaching judgments about domestic abuse and to take firm legal action against it.

This book is ordered so that early, after giving a historical context for domestic and sexual violence, you will be given help in determining the role this destructive dynamic plays in your life (Chapter 2). As you hold this present life situation in your awareness, you may work your way through your history and your sense of yourself (Chapter 5) which have determined your life to this point, and then through "A Course of Healing" (Chapter 6), which will provide you support to grow—to a better life. Chapter 7 offers a framework of values, self-examination, and growth exercises for couples undertaking change. It may also be helpful for you, as an individual, in setting your sites on developing a positive new relationship.

As you proceed, note practices and meditations that are particularly meaningful to you. As your life situation varies, the sections of this book that feel relevant may vary. The stage in your own healing will determine the kind of information that is most helpful. Allow yourself simplicity. If there is one idea or practice suggestion that feels important, you may stay with it for weeks. Copy it on a notepad, which you can carry with you for further work, or post a phrase you find helpful on your mirror. Whenever you stumble, return to the chapter on healing and find practices that now fit for you.

Read each practice and meditation thoughtfully and use the space provided (or separate paper) to draw or make notes. What, if any, meaning does a meditation hold for you? Can you think of a particular time when you felt this way? React to each practice: Do you agree? Does it anger you? Does it make you feel stronger? Write your reactions or decide to discuss it with a friend or therapist.

This book is designed as a companion with which you may interact. It creates a connection for you with others using it who share your situation. Share it with friends; find or start a support group. You have power within yourself, and there is also power in numbers. [Note: if two or more of you want to use this as a workbook, make sure you each have a copy so that your privacy is assured.]

A NOTE FOR PROFESSIONALS

If you are a therapist, counselor, or support group leader, this book may be used either as the focus of, or as an adjunct to, therapy. As a tool for groups, it may be helpful to use any one chapter with a group working on that particular focus. Individually, most exercises are also appropriate for an entire group, with discussion afterwards. Another technique for some groups would be for members to choose favorite pieces to share.

For use in individual therapy, it may be desirable to follow a client's lead in working on chapters or exercises of interest, but this depends on several variables, including the client's development as well as your theoretical orientation. Meditations read by you, the therapist, allow the client the benefit of full relaxation and safety. Practices done at your lead may provide necessary structure and/or motivation for the client. Processing time afterward may be valuable or even essential.

This book is applicable for work with couples who have never been physically violent or, if so, are beyond this. If couples are actively violent, this book can be used for the partners separately until they are ready for work together. Couples in verbally or emotionally abusive relationships will require willingness by both parties. Supportive encouragement for individual accountability will provide the basis for client/therapist collaboration.

PART TWO

THE CHALLENGE OF RELATIONSHIPS

There are many different styles of relationships; people in relationships come from various backgrounds and have differing interests, values, and expectations. This leaves plenty of room for confusion. Molding differences into a workable and loving unit can be quite challenging. Although all kinds of factors—from personality to religion to ethnicity to sexual orientation—will affect a relationship, the basic challenge that makes the difference between safety and danger is the fundamental need for mutual respect. This book focuses on those feelings, expressions, and behaviors that represent and instill respect or destroy it.

In spite of so many people in our culture experiencing stress and failure in their intimate relationships, I believe that relationships can work to the health and benefit of those who want them. If a relationship is desired only to meet one type of need—sexual or economic, for example—acknowledging this allows the relationship to be honestly measured by its participants. But for our purposes we will be dealing with the needs of an intimate relationship. Intimacy is multi-dimensional; that is, it is meant to connect people on many levels so as to produce emotional as well as physical security.

Safety and respect create a basis for intimate relationships that provide connection, security, growth, and enjoyment. Sex and the parenting of children may be included. Basically, relationships are meetings at the physical as well as spiritual level, and to be healthy they must be lived in respect and from the heart.

Problems in relationships can be seen on a continuum from subtle to obvious. Because one partner has never hit the other does not mean the relationship is free from domination. It is quite possible to have no physical abuse present for the very fact that the domination is total. However, if there is physical or sexual abuse, it is accurate to say that for the victim the relationship is life threatening. A history of sexual abuse may deter you from to asserting yourself as an adult in very life-threatening ways. A situation of physical threat or violence is a danger until the dominator learns physical self-control. There is no bargaining with this reality.

Physical abuse, however, is not the only behavior that destroys relationships. There are many destructive relationship dynamics, such as: criticism, denigration, humiliation, resentment, control, restriction, and many forms of manipulation.

The dominating of one person by a relationship partner is at the core of abuse. Domination in human sexual relationships has existed for as long as any of us knows. An old English law allowed a husband to beat or whip his wife, so long as the object he used was no wider than his thumb. This was the "Rule of Thumb." Even as recently as the early 1900s in the United States, an argument against women's right to vote was that the government should not interfere in a husband's right to handle, that is, punish his wife, because it would upset the balance of harmony in the home. To this day, the belief in "putting a woman in her place" is widely expressed either as blatant hostility or in anxious humor.

For centuries, ownership has also been an issue in relationships. Old English common law allowed that a man who killed his wife was doing away with his own property. (If a woman killed her husband, she would be killed for treason, her husband being considered the "king" of the manor.)

Even in the early 1970s in Texas and New Mexico, a man who killed his wife for committing adultery could claim justifiable homicide and be acquitted. Many states have intricately camouflaged routes of defense for men accused of murdering their wives. Their crime might be justified as the "heat of passion" in any number of ways. They might have been carried away by the moment, or conversely, they might have stored up anger over hours. A man could justify losing control immediately or over a long period of time. In comparison, women who have killed abusive husbands in self-defense, husbands who have abused them for years, continue to be treated harshly by the courts.

Over the past two decades, research on gay and lesbian relationships has shown that in these relationships, we continue to find patterns based upon domination and control. This allows us to see that although males have been the "owners" and controlling partners, intimate human relationships, regardless of gender issues, have had an important element of domination. We know that control and domination restrict growth, cause fear, passivity, rage, and illness in *both* participants.

Individuals can change themselves and thereby change a relationship. All abusive relationships do not need to end, but the abuse must. In order for change to occur, all avenues of self-protection must be opened. Alternative living arrangements may need to be made. It requires one person to initiate change, and it requires two to bring it about. The victim most often has the job of initiating change because the dominator is experiencing the reward of control.

Many books have focused on the need for victims to increase their self-esteem to initiate change. I take the approach that victims should seek direct help, from groups who treat abusive partners, the police, community leaders, and our courts. Someone trying to increase her or his self-esteem while being abused is up against a monumental task—not impossible perhaps, but extremely difficult. Do not set yourself up this way if you are in an abusive relationship. Get help for yourself. If your partner wants to get help, in time you may be able to achieve your goals. Do not wait for your self-esteem to lift to get help. Let your fear guide you in ways that build your protection and inner strength. For the sake of your life.

CHAPTER TWO

THE EYE OF THE STORM

HOW ABUSE LOOKS, ACTS, AND FEELS

If you have asked, pleaded, or told your partner to stop hurting you in some way, or if you have *been* asked, pleaded with, or told by your partner to stop hurting *them* in some way, you have both witnessed the scene of the storm.

If you "hope" it will never happen again, if you "can't believe" it ever happened in the first place, if you think it was "just the drinking," if you think it was "something different" than what we are referring to in this book, you are at one of the most important choice points in your life. Unless you choose a new course of behavior for yourself, "it" will happen again and, yes, it is abuse.

It may look ugly, tense, aggressive, or it may look cold, calm, and controlled. It may cry and look afraid; it may cower or run; it may shield its face or body; it may yell, strike back, or do nothing. It may look *very* innocent even on the face of the perpetrator. But if you are near it you can feel the tension. You can always feel it and you can always see it in the eyes of the people, in the eye of the storm.

In reading a book such as this, you are very likely someone who is attempting to put abuse behind you. But like many others, you need information about your experience and a new perspective to assure that you have beacons of light for safety along your new course. These beacons are mental and emotional cues that will provide order and boundaries for your relationships with others. Provide yourself with a fantasy or two of how you want your life to feel. Notice how it is different from your present life. Then begin defining the danger signals of trouble and gather life boats for your support.

If you have been abused, you are healed when you know that you can live outside the abuse; that you are a well-spring for your own health; that when you ask for connection with spiritual favor, you will receive it. It means that you live in safety with your loved ones and that you can control your reactions to others to assure that you will not hurt them, and they are not hurting you.

What Drives Abuse

There are many philosophical and religious views pertaining to abuse. What meaning should we give it? What causes it? Is abuse the result of a need for power or domination? Perhaps abuse is caused by innate tension between the sexes. Sociologists might assert that abuse is the result of economic factors or a culture that permits or even admires violent, sexist behavior. Or is abuse the negative side of the seemingly universal struggle between good and evil? If violence to others were an innate drive, it could never be resolved. If it were a symptom of the tension between the sexes, gay relationships would not involve abuse.

We know most violent behavior is learned. And abusiveness is certainly not limited to men. In fact, it may be as common in women, though expressed differently. In getting beneath the surface of questions about the cause of abuse, it is revealed to be the outcome of fear.

To understand the underlying cause of abuse, try the following exploration of your own emotional process:

Practice: Finding Your Fear

Clear your mind by taking a few easy, deep breaths. Think of something you ordinarily feel or recently felt upset or irritated about. Make this recollection strong so the situation is very clear to you.

Now consider that, in all your emotional reactions, you are in a state of either love or fear.

In your angry state, you may insist on believing anger is your only feeling, but experiment. Obviously, you are not in a state of love and well-being. Ask yourself what you fear. Do not settle for any answer that is a version or restatement of anger. Push yourself until you can identify underlying fear. For example, you may be afraid that you will be rejected or excluded by others. Perhaps you are afraid you will not be taken care of or are afraid of being judged.

See if the recognition of fear gives you ideas on how to deal differently with a situation than if you were to stay in anger.

Anger is a defense against many fears. The fear of loss is a powerful feeling that we often fail to recognize. Loss takes many forms. The ending of a relationship means loss of companionship, security, perhaps pleasure. It means loss of familiarity or certainty in our lifestyle. Change can be very threatening, particularly if we have others who are dependent upon us or if we are not prepared to support ourselves physically as well as emotionally.

One of our greatest, though subtle, fears is that we will be either disconnected from or never reach the place within ourselves that is expansive, joyful, meaningful—our creativity. If we look to other people to fill this inner space, we will have an endless sense of void.

In an abusive relationship, the abuser is futilely connected to his partner. As long as he has the opportunity to control and act out anger at his partner, he does not need to go deeper within himself and feel his fears. Intimacy requires joining with another person, forming a union that is different from either individual. Within this entity, the abused partner takes on the role of a punching bag, at times representing a part of the abuser, a part that he may hate because it is weak or fearful. At other times, the abused partner may represent someone who has hurt the abuser. An abusive partner is fearful, sometimes afraid just of the *feeling* of fear.

Particularly for men in their historical position of protecting themselves and their families (or any individual who identifies with this role), fear was a weakness that, if shown, could be life threatening. There were rituals, beliefs, and communal ways of dealing with fear that supported the warriors and protectors. In modern cultures, there is much less need for men to fill a basic protective function, yet at the same time, men (and women) experience pressures and expectations that they function competently and independently to provide for themselves or their families. This requires emotional rather than physical strength. To have emotional strength, a new system of supports must be in place. For men to be stronger in dealing with their fears, they can no longer succeed by "fighting it out."

In our section "A Word to Dominators," written for abusing partners, we will discuss methods that support men being emotionally stronger. To the vulnerable partner, we say that when you instill in your relationship the expectation that abuse can and will end, you provide support and strength to your partner. This gesture alone gives both of you the message that you are stronger than you are acting.

Physical Abuse: Patterns in Perpetuity Until You Change Them

Physical abuse is very recognizable. Usually, confusion about it stems from the victim's sense of denial. Physical abuse cannot be excused or explained in any way that would make it tolerable or acceptable.

You know absolutely if you are being physically abused. It is abuse if you are being pushed, grabbed, shoved, restrained, slapped, punched, kicked, bitten, choked, forced, hit by objects, pointed at or hurt by a weapon, chased, or run off the road. It is abuse if you are forced to have sex, spanked, or subjected to any other unwelcome, hurtful, or controlling physical act. Do not stay around someone who is doing this to you. If it is a pattern, do not remain in proximity to this person until they: (1) get help and/or (2) show great improvement. Even if you are with someone who has had an abusive pattern and is making significant progress, do not remain with them if they begin abusing again. For the sake of your life.

Practice: An Invitation to Join Others

If you are beginning to read this book and you are the victim of physical abuse in your relationship, this is an invitation to you. Work with all of us who are in a similar situation. Please feel this companionship.

In your imagination, picture a group and make yourself one of the members. Create a sense of support in this group: people are interested in each other and in you. Members are able to share information about themselves and care about each other's well-being. See yourself the way you may appear to others. You are attentive; you are present. This presence is all you need to grow in safety.

Be with this group in your imagination whenever you want. Use the members for feedback, creating supportive conversations with them. Accept their gifts of understanding and caring. (Joining such a group is discussed further in Chapter 4.)

Lastly, please accept the wishes throughout this book that are intended to make your life safer and more content.

Emotional Abuse: All Wrapped Up in Negative Emotions

We will deal with emotional abuse in more detail, to show ways to think about it as well as to give examples. It is important to know the difference between hurt and abuse. When we refer to abuse, there is a pattern of control that characterizes the abuser's behavior. On the other hand, hurt is at times an inherent aspect of intimacy. The first step in identifying emotional abuse is to take a close look at your relationships.

Practice: Assessing the Risk in Your Relationship

You know or feel physical abuse. Emotional abuse is more subtle and therefore difficult to identify. Many resource books will label abusive behavior for you, but you are also an important source of knowledge on the subject.

Examine your thoughts and your feelings toward your partner. Your answers to these questions may reveal the enduring quality of your relationship. The degree of positive or negative feeling you have is an indicator of the level of damage which has been done to it.

What do you like about your partner?

What do you dislike?

Do you trust your partner to be considerate of your needs?

For example: Together you are planning a trip and although you have a fear of flying, you have agreed to do so. But in order to have the greatest sense of security possible, you need to have plenty of time to get to the airport. Will your partner agree to plan for this? Or, on a more serious level, if you are recovering from a chemical addiction and find it difficult to be around people using a particular drug, will your partner agree to limit his use to times and places when he is not around you?

Think of examples in your own life, and how your partner could show consideration for your needs. When does this happen?

When does this not happen?

Are your feelings respected and taken seriously?

To answer, it may be helpful to think of something you like to do: for example, visiting with a friend, going to a place you like, exercising. If your partner regularly interrupts you and you request that he not do so, does he listen and respond to your request? Or, think of something you do not like: a particular food, a certain kind of activity. Does your partner accept this preference or does he cajole or in other ways try to change you? (We are not referring here to things you may want to change about yourself.)

When does your partner respect your feelings?

When does your partner not respect your feelings?

If you ask to be treated differently, what response do you receive?

An example may be the way you like or do not like to be touched. Once you have expressed your preference, your partner would change how he touches you.

When does this happen?

When does this not happen?

Is there give and take between you and your partner? In other words, do you yield to the other person's preferences at some times? And is your partner willing to yield to yours?

In what ways are you giving?

In what ways are you given to?

Name any trades you might negotiate, for example, an activity you would participate in with your partner in exchange for one your partner might do with you:

Do you make personal decisions for yourself?

You may or may not do this in small ways as well as more important ones. Will you buy a magazine just for yourself? Do you consider what you feel comfortable wearing, as opposed to what your partner wants you to wear? Do you feel free to consider returning to school if that is something you have wanted to do?

List any personal ways you are letting your partner control your decisions:

Do you hide or cover up your activities or other things about yourself in fear that your partner will judge, try to control, or punish you?

List anything you feel the need to hide:

There are times in any intimate relationship when tiredness or irritability causes exasperation, blaming, or expressions of anger. There are abusive behaviors for which we are all responsible. What identifies an emotionally abusive relationship, however, is a pattern which allows the other person to diminish you and to establish control over you. This may seem less severe than physical violence, and you might make excuses for your partner or minimize the danger to yourself. However, this abusive pattern, this abuse of your spirit, this abuse of your personal integrity is a direct attack upon your being. Saving yourself may be the most important job of your life.

Emotionally Destructive Patterns of Behavior

Does your partner behave like any of these characters? Do any of these patterns apply to your relationship?

The Character	Unspoken Message	The Effect
King of the Hill	"There will be no questioning my authority."	Totally dominating; totally disrespectful
The Peacock	"Everyone knows I'm better than you."	Degrading you by virtue of supposed superiority
Head Honcho	"You will do everything I want, how I want, when I want."	Controlling you by demanding, ordering
The Know-It-All	"The way I see it is right."	Discounting you with intellectual snobbery
The Critic	"You don't know what you're talking about."	Demeaning you by criticizing
The Center-Stager	"I want all the attention; yours and everyone else's."	Diminishing you by ignoring your needs
The Two-Year-Old	"I always get what I want, and I want it now."	Unreasonably demanding and making you pay a price if he does not get what he wants

The Total Companion	"I want you all to myself."	Suffocating: demanding openly or subtly that you give up your own friends or activities to devote yourself to his
The Power-Player	"You will if I say so." by threatening reprisal	Demanding compliance
The Strong, Silent Type	"I carry a big stick, so I don't need to say anything." (This could be literal as in fist, weapon.)	Instilling fear
The Hold-Out	"I can last longer than you can."	Withholding to punish or manipulate you
Too Tough to Fool With	"My anger will let you know how tough I am."	Intimidating you by yelling to make you compliant
The Saboteur	"I'll say yes to your face, but watch your back."	Undermining
The Cold Fish	"If you don't do what I want, I'll freeze you out."	Emotionally isolating to hurt or control you
The Put-Down Artist	"*You've* got the problem. I'm okay."	Criticizing to undermine your self-confidence

In spiritual terms, you must save yourself from these kinds of diminishment. Furthermore, you must not provide the opportunity for someone to behave toward you in patterns of behavior like these.

Practice: The Screenplay

Refer to the characters just described under "Emotionally Destructive Patterns of Behavior." Begin describing the character in your real life screenplay, your partner. Use a name or names to suit the person.

What phrase best describes their personal style?

Note if any of the characters describes your own behavior.

Verbal Violence

Physical and emotional abuse are often accompanied by verbal abuse. We all know it and very likely experienced it as children. On the playground, at the beach, or in the car, it was taunting, name calling, teasing, cat calls, friends whispering nasty remarks behind your back, or worse. The style of abuse to which children and adolescents are exposed in present society is more vicious and physically oriented, partly due to the mass media as well as the development of gang mentality and the availability of drugs and weapons. For those struggling in abusive adult partnerships, it is not hard to recognize the painfulness and destructiveness of verbal abuse.

As with any form of abuse, verbal denigration serves the purpose of one partner controlling and dominating the other. If you look beyond the bluff and bluster, you can see that this person is presuming the right to usurp your self-direction. In a very real sense, a claim is being made against your personal as well as spiritual wholeness.

If you are being abused, it is most important for you to recognize it. What we are able to identify may be changed more easily.

Verbal Ways to Denigrate

We all know a dirty mouth, a hostile mouth, and sometimes we can spot a deceitful mouth. These mouths are all violent, of course. So are mouths that yell, call names, and spew out anger or disgust. There are many more subtle ways to hurt another person verbally:

Blaming: "If it weren't for you, I would…be successful."
"…be calm."
"…be kind."
"…*not* have broken the chair."
"…*not* have hit you."

"You make me angry."

"You are the cause of my…gaining weight."
"…swearing."
"…impatience."

Attacking: "You said that wrong."

"You shouldn't have done that."

Mind Control: "You don't mean that."

"I know you don't feel that way."

Criticizing: "You're too…serious."
"…sensitive."
"…twisted."
"…hostile."
"…greedy."

Undermining: "You probably couldn't pass the test."

"You wouldn't really fit in there."

Joking: "With a nose like yours, you have to wear a big hat."

"If *you* drive, you'll never get there."

A note about humor: Human foibles and idiosyncrasies can be entertaining and are often endearing. It can be a relief not to take ourselves too seriously. But you know in your heart if something is said warmly, or cruelly.

Practices on Understanding Abuse

From this chapter, you may have already identified people and patterns in your life that have been abusive. It is essential to your moving forward that you do so because you have been affected by your past. You may choose a partner who is like an abusive parent. Or one who is the opposite.

The following practices provide opportunities to focus clearly. Writing is a good way to strengthen yourself because it gives you perspective and control.

Practice: Logging On (Setting Up Information from Your History)

Note the people you have chosen as friends and any kind of abusive dynamic in each relationship:

Was one person in control of the other?

Did one person bully the other?

Were there put-downs?

Did one person always get their way?

Did one person raise their voice or intimidate with threats?

Practice: On Not Accepting Blame

The idea that victims "get what they ask for" has quite a demeaning tone to it, as does blaming the victim for staying with an abusive partner. This is sometimes expressed by saying, "Why doesn't she leave?" Therapeutic programs for abusers have begun to address the question, "Why doesn't he stop beating her?" You must not be side-tracked by the effect of any of these expressions or questions. You will learn not to accept blame.

For now, note what you are doing about your situation. Examples may be:

reading this book

labeling abuse

talking to others about your situation

Practice: "Out-Of-Control" is *In Control*

A common myth about abusive partners is that their abuse occurs as a result of loss of control. Abusers are really very much in control insofar as they know when they can "get away with" putting down, hitting, or in other ways being violent.

Have you seen your partner speak or act unacceptably toward you and then suddenly become nice to others? Or perhaps hit you, then answer the door and act as if everything is fine? Write down examples of this kind of behavior.

Have you considered that this behavior change requires self-control? You must choose to clearly see the information you have. If your partner's behavior is described above, you are at high risk: in the first instance, for emotional abuse, and in the second, for serious on-going physical abuse. You must think carefully about your safety. You must begin seeking support and help outside your relationship. This is a choice point for you, and you can guide your life in a new direction.

Meditation: Creating New Expectations

There is a common belief that "victims ask for what they get." We consider this a myth, but a deeper level of dynamic does seem to exist. It is quite true that, if we are *afraid* of another person treating us harmfully, we have entered into an emotional zone that makes the negative behavior more likely. When you are in fear, you are in a state of expectancy. You can change this.

Take a few minutes to relax. Think of something, even if slight, that you enjoy. Anticipate this. Picture it; recall the taste of it or the sense of doing it. Savor this. Look forward to it. Experience this state of expectancy that you are in—it is positive; you have a sense of well-being. By learning the control you have of your expectations, you have done the same thing that is required to begin to turn your life around.

Practice: Seeking Positives

If you are in an abusive relationship, do not consider yourself a failure. If you have left and returned to abuse, it is because you have lessons to learn. If you leave abuse and do not return, you are growing into a new future and will reap many rewards. The relationships in your life represent a new future. Align yourself with people who can help you become who you want to be.

Think of a friend or associate you feel trust in and think of how they behave toward you. Note these traits or behaviors. For example: "I trust Ann because she is honest with me."

Which of these traits or behaviors do you recognize in yourself?

CHAPTER THREE

AFTER-EFFECTS: REACTIONS TO ABUSE

Abuse can have several effects on one's personality. These "after-effects," as we call them, are difficult to change because they have served the valuable purpose of defense. The defenses of disbelief, dissociation, or depression may have shielded you from emotional hurt, physical pain, or perhaps even from experiencing the collapse of your family. But while helping you hold your life together, these defenses also have prevented you from fully acknowledging the abuse that is occurring or kept you so busy coping that you have been unable to establish self-sufficiency in your life.

These defenses are part of the broader spectrum of reactions to abuse called post-traumatic stress disorder, or PTSD. This term was used clinically after it became apparent that soldiers presented particular symptoms after experiencing the horrors of war. Women with histories of sexual abuse had been presenting these symptoms for years. You may recognize PTSD by the jumpiness and looking around (hypervigilance) by someone (or yourself) who has just been beaten. You may be experiencing PTSD if you experience loss of sleep because nightmares awaken you. Or you may have discomforting memories or images which you may or may not know the source of. You may have a chronic feeling of emptiness or constant uneasiness around people. Other signs of PTSD include difficulty concentrating or remembering, isolating from others, or hurting yourself. A particularly subtle symptom could be described as living two lives at once: the life lived during the time of your trauma is always present in your mind as is your current life. The effect of this has wide-ranging ramifications as the reliving of the past takes away energy you would normally have available to invest in the present. Two excellent books on PTSD, should you want more information, are *Trauma and Recovery* by Judith Herman, M.D., and *Trust After Trauma* by Aphrodite Matsakis, Ph.D.

This chapter describes and works with the major defenses of denial, dissociation, and depression. These dynamics go hand-in-hand with the symptoms of PTSD. For example, self-mutilation or injury would not occur without accompanying dissociation or depression. Your healing process is going to involve working through defenses to recover your life.

In the case of disbelief (or denial), the *awareness* that could stimulate action is blocked. Dissociation, the second defense, blocks feelings, thus interfering with your motivation to take action. With depression, your energy is subdued, hindering your ability to take action.

Disbelief: Blocked Awareness

"I don't believe it." "You can't be serious." These phrases reflect the powerful ability we have to create in our minds a world we can cope with. We "deny" those things that we do not understand or wish to accept. This may include behaviors of our friends, life's perversities or horrors, unpleasant aspects of our partner or ourselves. You may want to believe your partner is a kind person, that abusive behavior is just an aberration, an exception to who they really are. You may want to believe you are not being used or abused. It is important to see the positive qualities in ourselves and in others. Abusive behavior does not describe everything about another person any more than being the object of abuse describes all of who you are.

To replace denial gradually, it will be helpful to take your work in steps. You may love your partner and want the relationship to continue. If this is the case, your desire can actually motivate you to demand an end to abuse. You must have a bottom line and your life may be that line. Whether you want an end to your relationship or not, you must believe that abuse does not have to be allowed. If you are in grave danger, as many women are if they try to leave an abusive partner, you must work first and foremost on building a support system. No matter what your situation, you are in more danger if you are in denial because you will not be finding your way to safety. Once you know that help is at hand—from friends, a women's shelter, a support group—you will be better able to work at ending your denial and preserving your life.

Practice: Wishful Thinking

One form of disbelief or denial is wishful thinking. It is a way we unknowingly deny the obvious. For example, "I'll believe him, if he'll say he won't hit me again." You may actually have explained repeated abuse by saying, "I wanted to believe him." This is a false belief— wishful thinking—because it does not have a basis in reality.

Recall a time when you told yourself something you wanted to believe about your partner, something you later learned not to be true. Write down the false belief and then write down the more accurate one.

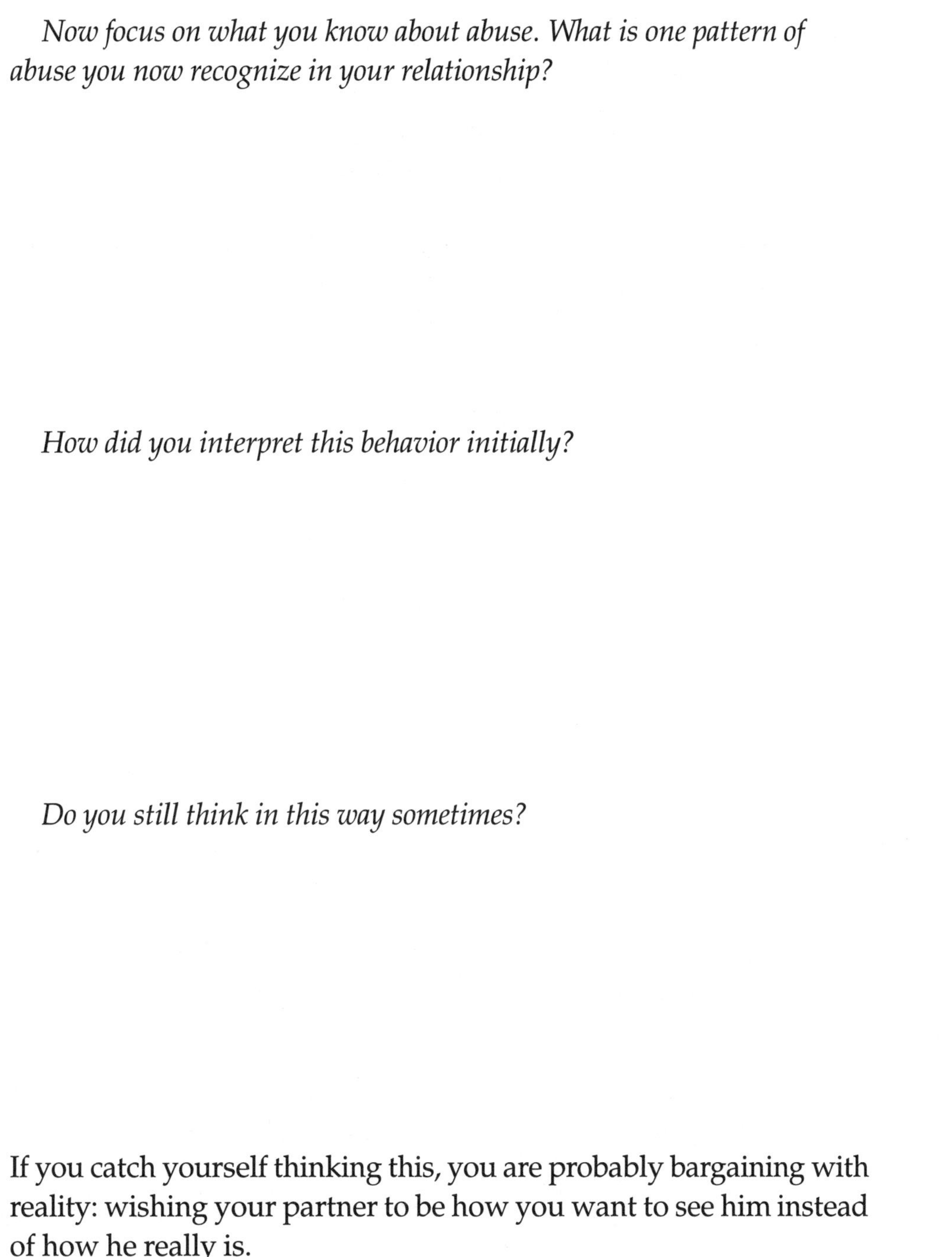

Now focus on what you know about abuse. What is one pattern of abuse you now recognize in your relationship?

How did you interpret this behavior initially?

Do you still think in this way sometimes?

If you catch yourself thinking this, you are probably bargaining with reality: wishing your partner to be how you want to see him instead of how he really is.

Practice: When "There's a Reason" (Drinking, Drugs, Just Lost His Job, Bad Childhood)

Often times, abuse is obvious, but we state a reason for it that serves as an excuse. This is a form of denial; it is a cover-up. We are each responsible for *all* of our actions. If your partner is abusive when he drinks, he is responsible both for the abuse and the drinking. If he always has a reason, he is responsible both for the abuse and for making excuses. It is hurtful to you to make excuses for your partner.

List excuses you might be making.

Practice: The Gardening Method of Creating Your Fantasy Partner—Selective Memory

Another form of disbelief or denial is selective memory. In a new relationship, this is a process of "weeding out" things that would not appeal to you or "planting in" qualities you want to exist. This is a way of creating your ideal (fantasy) partner out of a mere human. The more unclear you are in your own identity, the more this dynamic will occur.

Recall meeting your partner. Note events that occurred between you that you chose to ignore.

Note qualities you told yourself he had that were based on what you wanted, but were not accurate about him.

Selective memory can be an important aspect of choosing a partner who becomes abusive.

Dissociation: Blocked Motivation

The term "dissociation" is used in psychology to describe one form of emotional protection, a way of stepping aside, stepping outside of yourself. A non-feeling front stands in for you to allow you to "take" an experience, the way a boxer's mouthpiece is put in place to cushion his teeth from blows. Dissociation helps protect you from being shattered, hurt, or overwhelmed by terror or pain. But dissociation that prevents you from these experiences can also lead to blocking your motivation to change.

We hear dissociation referred to when someone describes being in an accident and feeling that the experience seemed unreal. The person knew what had happened, but a "letting go" mechanism took over to the extent that a near-dream state was created. We hear of dissociation in accounts of surgery when an anesthesia-induced euphoria gave the patient the sense of watching the process from the ceiling. In spiritual terms, this can occur quite naturally as an "out-of-body" experience. Most of us have also heard of Multiple Personality Disorder, more recently called Dissociative Identity Disorder. This is an extreme situation wherein the defense of stepping aside creates new personalities as stand-ins. The need for relief is so acute that separating from the self must occur to preserve coping. A milder form of this can be seen in the Imposter Syndrome, when a person is so separated from themselves, and therefore their talents, that they feel like a "fake" if they succeed. Many of us experience mild dissociation when anxiety is triggered, for example, while giving a performance or challenging ourselves in a physical competition.

Dissociation is a serious concern whenever it reinforces itself and becomes a personal pattern. In this case, memory of the actual events that caused dissociation has been lost. Reasonable challenges and difficulties allow us to develop different aspects of our personalities. In this way, we acquire not only depth, but a variety of coping mechanisms, as well. In the case of abuse, however, if a style of dissociation has evolved, you may have lost contact with that part of yourself that needs to be present to change your situation. Motivation to change is energized by feeling, but an absent self cannot register the feelings ordinarily accompanying a traumatic event. It is for this reason that we have included many meditations and exercises in this book to help you become familiar with your feelings. Stepping back into your self is vital for change, and with change comes your healing.

Practice: How Absent Has Your Self Been?

To say that your self is "absent" is not saying you have no self. There is no such thing as being without a self. If you recognize "absenteeism" as a part of your problem, this knowledge provides you with a focus for work in reconnecting with yourself.

The following are some signals that you may have developed an "absent" self:

> When you are with others, you ask them to decide where to go, what to do, when to do it, because you do not know what you want. If someone asks you your likes and dislikes, you do not know. There are things that many people know, like what kind of house or partner they want, and you do not know.

Ask a friend to describe you. Describe yourself in even the most basic ways. Make several statements about yourself. Please do not avoid this practice.

Practice: Learning Your Coping Style

When you developed a pattern of dissociation, you did so for a reason. Something was the problem, not you. If there is one thing in your life you can change that is the most important of all, it will be to recognize:

- *What* was going on
- *What* behavior you developed to cope
- *What* purpose this served
- *What,* if anything, still requires this behavior of you

What was going on? Did your parents fight? Were people picking on you? Was there war? Illness? Death? Was there sexual activity you wanted to block out? What were the situations that disturbed your sense of safety?

What coping behavior did you develop? Were you a "jokester," always breaking the tension by cracking a joke? Were you a "good kid," being the first to yield, comply, be submissive? Were you a disappearing act, able to spin into activity, diversions, fantasy, at the hint of the problem situation occurring? List the particular behaviors you developed in an attempt to cope with problems.

What purpose was your behavior created to serve? Did it diffuse hostility? Did you think it would keep your father from hitting your mother or keep someone from abusing you? Did you think it would keep someone from drinking? What were you trying to accomplish?

When and why do you still do this behavior?

When and why (if ever) do you still need to do this behavior?

Note: Use this practice, take a break, return to it if you are not finished. It may take weeks on and off to complete, or it may be complicated enough that you seek professional help with it. Do what you can.

Depression: Blocked Energy

Depression may sound like the most serious reaction to abuse. It certainly feels debilitating and can threaten one's life if it leads to thoughts of suicide. It can also be life threatening if it creates a situation where you experience yourself as helpless. In such a state, your lack of caring for yourself can lead you to take chances or persist in dangerous situations.

Depression can be eased in a number of ways. First, following a description of some of the causes and characteristics of depression, a few simple practices are included in this chapter to help you identify how depression might be working in and on your life.

How to Spot Depression and What to Do About It

There are three main ways of understanding different causes of depression. One is *biological* or genetic, and if you have such a predisposition that you can identify in your family tree, you will be more vulnerable to situational and emotional factors that also cause depression.

Situational factors include events that occur around you or happen to you. Examples would include: war; lack of sunlight (which causes Seasonal Affective Disorder); birth of a child (Post-partum Depression); loss of job; death or illness of you or a family member; accident or injury; financial mishap or poverty; and lack of opportunity to change incapacitating circumstances (including being able to use your intelligence or other talent).

Emotional factors that cause depression are much more difficult to quantify or define because they often depend solely on personal history. That is, some people may feel undervalued in our culture for not measuring up to what a parent wanted them to achieve. Others doing the same activity but having had proud and supportive parents may feel content with their progress in life. This can generally be referred to as self-esteem, but it originates from so many sources and can exist or not in so many ways as to be quite idiosyncratic or unique to any one person.

But there *are* ways of viewing one's life that we know are characteristic of people who are and are not depressed. The *reasons* for these different cognitive sets (personal mindsets) vary greatly but not the sets themselves. You will be able to define these things yourself once you become aware of them. For example, think of someone who usually sees the positives in a given situation—what can be referred to as seeing the full half of the glass rather than the empty half. Or think of someone who industriously goes about trying to solve problems rather than giving up. Or the person who can state their needs to others versus someone who always backs down.

These people have a mindset that life can give to them, that they have the ability to change or create life circumstances and to act on behalf of themselves. We know these mindsets exist in people who are not generally depressed. Whereas a person who feels trapped, defeated, discouraged, useless, is hardly one who is motivated to act assertively. Their mindset or world view is negative and depressing. Many people whom we refer to as victims carry these mindsets. They have *learned* patterns of seeing themselves in relation to others. These patterns usually are learned by children and carry over into all later behavior unless or until they are relearned. This is why an adult who has been abused as a child often finds herself in negative personal relationships: she has learned to see relationships as hurtful, to expect this, to have behaviors (like self-depreciation) that attract dominating partners, and to tolerate people and situations that hurt her. This is not to say victims enjoy being hurt. We all grow up highly influenced by what we are taught, what we experience, and what we see around us as children. We all have to relearn many things as our world and life situation changes.

Many of us feel angry at the thought of people acting like "victims." Perhaps this is because we have all felt frustration and anger as infants and children when we were helpless or overpowered, controlled, and punished in the process of growing up. If we could only all have compassion for these conditions we might not be so blaming of adults who have continued to feel intimidated by life and by other people. Perhaps it is too life threatening for us to acknowledge our inherent human fragility. But in every moment that each of us can feel kindness and compassion for those who have a harder struggle than we, a bit more of a burden will be taken off the job of growing up and growing out of destructive patterns that most of us have to some degree. Depression is the carrying of heavy burdens, and these burdens are only increased when we are accused of being at fault for having them. With help, however, we can all learn to take responsibility for changing. The key to depression is to seek help in making changes.

There are many signs that would indicate to a therapist that you are depressed: teariness; chronic tiredness; inability to sleep or sleeping too much; irritability; inability to eat or eating too much; lack of interest in things outside yourself; inability to concentrate; having a negative attitude. If you are aware of your feelings, you may realize that you feel down, blue, suicidal, or dislike yourself or others. Some people who are depressed get down on themselves for being depressed.

There is no end to the power depression can have over your life. But depression now is like polio since the Salk vaccine, or a number of other physical disease states that we have immunization for.

There are many different healing approaches including medication, light therapy, physical exercise, nutritional intervention, and a variety of meditational processes. Get help and get a referral for the kind of intervention that appeals to you. But get help!

The following exercises are written to help you connect abuse dynamics to depression. (A thorough, general book for this purpose is *Feeling Good* by David Burns.) Use the exercises to understand better what you are dealing with and to counter any shame you may associate with being depressed.

Practice: Which to Attend to First: Depression or Your Relationship

Situational depression means you are reacting to a relatively current situation and feeling depressed about it. Long-term depression (dysthymia) means you may have chosen a partner who fits into a depressing view that you have of life.

Remember how you used to be. Which came first:

A long-term feeling that limited your ability to enjoy things, that sometimes kept you from having the energy to be involved actively in your life, feeling badly about yourself, your body, your personality, or your abilities;

or

your partner?

It is important to know who you were when you chose your partner. If you were depressed first, you may need to seek help for depression first. If you were not depressed until abuse from your partner began, you have more leeway as to whether you deal with your relationship or depression first. Either way, expect your view of your relationship to change.

Practice: One Step at a Time

If you are depressed, one of the best things you can do is acknowledge it. This provides you the focus to: (1) get help, and (2) improve your self-care.

Take one step for the care of your inner or outer self: Make a list of possible choices so that you can refer to this list when you need to and add to it when you learn what makes you feel better. Some areas to consider:

Nutrition

Exercise

Time with people

Working with this book

Establishing privacy and keeping a journal

Practice: Depression Can Make a Waste of Life

Steps you can take if an abusive relationship is depressing you or if depression is allowing you to stay in one:

Acknowledge depression.

Get professional help for depression.

Find help to prepare yourself to confront the abuse (call community services, women's shelters, etc.).

Establish a safety plan. If you are in a threatening situation, you need resources that you can turn to in order to be safe.

Let your partner know: Prepare a time and place and what you want to say to your partner. You may rehearse with a friend or write it down. Give your partner time to respond. This may mean days. But do not tolerate threats or put downs for having given voice to your feelings.

List the steps you will take and the resources available to you:

Practice: Learning Depression

Being treated abusively teaches you unworthiness. Being controlled teaches you powerlessness. Although different, each causes depression.

(a) *Think of the things your partner says to you that hurt your feelings, make you angry, or in some other way make you feel bad. Write a few of these down.*

(b) *Now write any of these same things you tell yourself and how you say them.*

(c) *Now write down why you think they are true.*

(d) *Did someone tell you these same things when you were a child? If not, how else might you have come to believe them?*

(e) *Now name some reasons they might not be true.*

For example, your list might look like this:

(a) *"You're lazy."*

(b) *"I'm lazy."*

(c) *"I'm lazy because I have to force myself to do things that other people seem to have the natural energy for."*

(d) *"My mother told me I was lazy."*

(e) *"What I call laziness could be depression. My husband nags me to clean like my mother did. I feel controlled and angry about this."*

Practice: Breaking in a New Path

Depression has a voice of its own. It resides in a room with many doors. When you hurt, it might say, "I'm just feeling sorry for myself." Feel your pain and open the door to another room that says, "I hurt" or "I feel sad for the pain I had." Nudge this door farther and farther open. You may see that there are two rooms: one contains the voice of depression, the other the voice of compassion. Notice the words depression uses to speak. Compare these to expressing words of compassion for yourself. Go back and forth from room to room until the path is well-worn and you can easily put the words of depression back in their room and choose from the room of compassion. Now, "I'm stupid" may change to "I have limits." "I'm demanding" may change to "I want to meet my needs." "I don't deserve" may change to "I'm precious." "I have to be perfect to make up for my faults" may change to "I'm human. I have faults. I'm normal."

Note other ways in which you can restate a depressed, negative sense of yourself into positive statements.

CHAPTER FOUR

BEGINNING TO HEAL

ON THE ORDER OF THINGS

We have discussed generally some of the ways human relationships are viewed. We are dealing with a difficult subject, the most unattractive facet of behavior: abuse. The scene of the storm is ugly. Emotional, verbal, and physical abuse are abhorrent. They are devastating and hurtful, causing disbelief, dissociation, and depression. We know abuse is spiritually reprehensible. It can even result in death.

We have recast this difficult subject not only with mandates for change but with opportunity for healing and growth. This chapter will lay a foundation for you as you move forward in this process.

For you to begin, the importance of linking up with others will be emphasized. If you have been abused, you have likely kept the secrets and shame to yourself. After you have acknowledged and labeled abusive behavior in your relationship, you must have support so that you are not dependent totally upon someone who is abusing you. Hopefully, you know a source for spiritual support, but to navigate the changes ahead you need human support, as well.

Moving from Isolation to Connection

The need for contact with other people does not mean that if you are quiet you need to become outgoing; if you are introverted you should develop a multitude of friendships; or if you consider yourself the life of the party, you can't need help. Connection is not about numbers and neither is isolation. Many of us have had the experience of feeling very lonely while among a group of people or at a social gathering. And connection is not necessarily about intimacy. We can establish belonging in a group of others seeking change in their intimate relationships. We can have a position of membership in the group by attending its meetings. We can have connection to other members simply by having the same interest. Many of us think of connecting with such a group as a situation of having to be liked by others, forgetting that our linkage with them is not about popularity but about mutual support and problem solving. And many of us think of joining such a group in terms of having great ideas to offer, and forget to be open to what others are asking for. If we are afraid to join with others for help in changing, it is often because of some false belief we have of what others will expect of us. And of course this fear can also stem from shame about having needs.

You may also be afraid to join with others because of negative experiences you have had with groups in the past. You may be forgetting that if you are in a group to seek change, asking other group members to help is part of what they are there for. This is a major move for you to make and it is one that truly teaches mutuality. If you are seeking help in establishing mutuality, cooperation, and give and take in your relationships, your effort to join a group may be the first step.

Practice: Experimenting with Connection

If joining a group or asking for help is a big stumbling block for you, and you know this, you are one step along the way. Set a goal for yourself depending on where you are in your process:

Just attend a group meeting of any kind.

Go to a class and ask a question

Attend a learning or skills development class and help someone do something you have already learned how to do

After a group meeting, journal what you were thinking about

If you were preoccupied with yourself, set a goal for your next meeting: Write down the subject you are interested in and continually bring your attention back to this.

Learn from watching others but also take risks. Be gentle with your assumptions about any group and be gentle with suggestions. When you are new to a group, you may ask questions to clarify the purpose of the group or how things are usually done, or confusions about how you would fit in or how the group would help you.

A group can be any number of people and have any number of purposes. It can be a friendship group of three. It can be formal, with a set time, place to meet, and function. Or it can be as informal as a coffee break. It can be casual but appointed as in a bowling league. There is no end to the opportunities to try on new behaviors because the dynamics of domination or mutuality will occur in every interaction you have.

Practice: Creating Belonging

You may not know what "family" feels like. Be free to create feelings of connection that you want and need with the people around you who support your growth. You can create a kind of "family" with your own friends if relatives are not supportive.

Who are your "chosen" family members?

What kind of contact with them do you value?

How might you celebrate holidays if friends or relatives are not available?

What do you need to be able to count on from your "chosen" family?

Proceeding to Your Personal Power

Developing personal power is as important as attaining power from connection with others. The meditations in this section will help strengthen your self-reliance. They can also help dispel depression and redirect tendencies of dissociation. By "associating" with yourself you can build a friendship system within, expanding and enlivening your personal identity.

There are two dangers to point out as you begin this work. One is that you become embittered. You may naturally feel angry, but allowing this energy to consume you will impede your growth. Proceed in your strength to acknowledge abuse that is occurring.

A second hazard is for you to let depression go unattended and to let it envelop you, cutting you off from healing. If you experience depression for more than a few weeks—or immediately if you sink to suicidal despair—seek the help of a trained mental health professional.

The following meditations take you through a series of steps, each providing you access to a different place within you. Overall, these meditations are offered to help you "center," a term describing the temporary ability to escape from activities, worries, and thoughts about your daily life and focus on yourself—your needs, your feelings, your abilities. For some people, this can be difficult and even uncomfortable. Physical or emotional feelings that are new or confusing to you may surface. For example, you may feel frightened or vulnerable. This is not uncommon. You may be particularly sensitive to such feelings to the degree that you have experienced abuse.

There are two important things to recall as you go through this book, and particularly as you go through these meditations. Do not proceed alone any further than is comfortable. Methods for you to experience your strength will be incorporated, but it takes time to feel confident. These meditations are offered to enable you to experience safety within yourself as well as for you to get to know yourself. This knowledge and assurance is what you must carry with you to meet your world and function safely in your relationships. Centering in yourself is a first step.

Practice: Easy Breathing—The Eight-Count Exercise

Many people have never realized that they can only appreciate the flavors of their food when they are breathing out or exhaling. Many of us are very tuned out of our natural functions. And the more stressful or abusive our experience has been, the more we learn to tune out. When we are tense or frightened, breathing is the first function to change, becoming shallow and constricted. All other physical functions follow from this: tight breathing and tight muscles cause physiological changes. Emotional changes occur also: we can become numb to our bodies as well as to our feelings. To heal, we need all our natural resources, but especially to heal emotional pain.

As you practice the following breathing exercise, be patient and gentle with yourself. It has taken you many years to form the breathing habits you have and it will take time to change these. Give yourself time to learn to do this exercise with comfort and until you have a feeling of well-being after doing it.

Do this exercise anywhere, anytime. Your only focus should be letting go of tension. Be still and in a comfortable position.

Breathe in slowly to the count of eight. Exhale to the count of sixteen.

Do this ten times.

As you practice you will learn to adjust your rate of breathing. You may change the number, for example, beginning with the count of one to breathe in and two to exhale. Build up to at least eight. The number can change but should be doubled as you exhale.

Associating with Your Self: A Basic Meditation in Four Parts

In learning to relax and open yourself to healing, breathing exercises are helpful. You may choose to continue these even for years. For now, becoming aware of your breathing, as in the Eight-Count Exercise, allows you to acquire the focus necessary to move forward. In the first part of the next section called *Loosening: A Meditation for Relaxing,* let the suggested images soothe you. Choose to focus on the words or phrases that help you achieve a sense of well-being or an uplifted feeling. Be patient and go slowly. If you are distracted, notice where your mind is directed and simply return to the meditation. If you feel tension, notice where it is and breathe gently to let go of the tension or soften it. Simply learning to relax can take time, but small successes along the way will help ease tension.

The meditations after *Loosening* build on each other in complexity. As you become sensitive to your breathing and able to begin relaxing, the meditations become more suggestive and use a greater variety of images. Healing involves breathing and relaxing, as well as controlling and creating your thoughts. If something is unhelpful or distracting, omit or change the wording so that you can proceed more easily.

Working on these meditations entails designating time and finding a place where you will not be interrupted. Often, this in itself is a challenge and can act as a first step to establishing a feeling of independence.

Record the entire meditation on tape, have a friend read it, or go over it in your mind until you remember it.

Loosening: A Meditation for Relaxing

Sit comfortably and close your eyes. Loosen, slowly…your breath moving through you, the brightness of sun glistening all around you. Let the light warm you and spread gently through your body. Imagine yourself becoming peaceful and aware. Breathe deeply; experience fullness. Let energy flow inward and outward, expanding, surrounding, and strengthening you. Light within shines toward everything around you and returns to you brighter. Find your place of comfort. Experience your wholeness. See the light intensify and energize you. You are Light. You are Life. You are your Greater Self.

Filling: A Meditation for Safety

Imagine in your mind a place of great beauty. Be there now. Bring with you warmth and peacefulness. If you are on a beach, what is it you love? The smell of the water; the warmth of the sun; the feeling of sand under your feet; a particular view. What do you hear? Or, if you are in the woods, what are the trees around you; the land; the flowers.... Is there water? Perhaps you are near a stream, a waterfall, or a cave. Create this place of beauty and notice, as an artist would, the things around you that you like. As you feel safe here, picture something that represents strength and protection to you: a magical potion, a gem, a spiritual presence, an animal, a song, a shaman, a posture. Draw it to you and quietly describe it to yourself. In your mind's eye, cherish and deepen this image. Feel its strength surrounding you; feel your body heighten, your face lift. As you breathe, fill over and over with new expanses of power. Fill...and release...fill...and release.... Imagine yourself as one with a greater source. Connect with your Power.
You are your Greater Self.

Feeling: A Meditation for Getting in Touch

Recall the peaceful feeling of loosening in the warmth of the sun. Again let light move through you and around you, warming your being. Experience light surrounding you; let your body wash with relaxation. Cherish a feeling of strength and draw your special power object near. Soften…welcome your power source, knowing you can draw it to you anytime you are uncomfortable. Feel protection build around you and color a fortress of silver white light in a circle around you. Begin to feel your body move within this fortress as a newborn stirs in its mother's soft cradling arms. Stretch…breathe…grow into your body as it is now. With each breath bring the sun into your chest, breathing in and out, loosening, glowing.

Wash yourself in green light, directing healing to any place of need in your body. Bring the color of pink roses to your heart…feel the kindness that resides there. Rest with this…extend this gentleness to your Self and to others. Erase any tension from your body as you direct light to your face. Loosen your arms, and guide light through your body. Pause with each breath to be aware of the energy of life within you. Let light embrace you as you stretch from head to toe, bathing in a sense of wholeness in your physical being. Feel the alertness of senses in your body, a resource of energy, health, and pleasure. Embrace yourself with positive feeling for what is given you in your body. Soften…cradle your body as a treasure. Be one with your body. Be one with your energy. You are your Greater Self.

Focusing: A Meditation For Action

Sit comfortably and close your eyes. Recall the peaceful feeling of loosening in the warmth of the sun. Spread yellow light throughout your body and draw your power object near. Intensify your brightness...focus on your power source. Begin to form an idea of something you wish to accomplish: building a flower garden; learning to drive; a new job; a healthier body; a painting; a degree.... Let go of all worry. Picture your wish, taking all the time you need, and when you are ready, draw it on a small billboard. Describe it; describe you; note the qualities or characteristics you bring to this goal. In your mind, place this billboard a hundred feet ahead of you on the rise of a slight hill. It may look like a goal, a mile marker, or a stage.

Now picture yourself standing back where you began, feet placed squarely, chest full, head high. Feel energy lifting you above the ground, your eyes focusing intently on the goal, an expression of confidence on your face. Picture this Self and fill every aspect of your posture with positive feeling and confidence. Look again at your goal; trace the outline; brighten the colors. Place yourself in the picture and describe to yourself how it feels to be there: soothed; stimulated; competent; active; creative.... Reach for your picture. Feel your arms and heart extend to encompass it. Claim it as your own. Now bring sun and power to your chest, filling with the feeling of the confidence you pictured on your face. Feel a spiral of light moving, energizing, actualizing within as you become part of your billboard. Experience joy in your accomplishment. You are one with your power. You are one with your goal. You are your Greater Self.

CHAPTER FIVE

WALKING THE PATH OF CHANGE ON YOUR OWN

Healing and changing are hard work, made much easier if done with help. If you were left alone as a child to deal with the trauma of abuse, you probably believe you have to do everything else alone, too. This is one of the biggest hurdles to your healing because healing involves learning to trust others enough to receive help. But trust in others develops at the same rate that we learn trust in ourselves, in our own feelings and actions.

You may have learned to trust in your defenses, to trust in avoidance, to trust even in depression. Everyone protects themselves with an outer self, but if you have been abused, you may have established such heavy reliance on an exterior self that your inner self is deeply buried. This "inner self" includes our "spiritual self." We have also referred to it in the four-part meditation as your "Greater Self." One problem with trusting in the exterior self is that she or he is separated from your heart. Your spiritual self, the part of you that requires protection, is your heart. A life lived without the heart is one full of grief. To address this grief, the path of healing can be lined with moments of peace, humor, companionship. Life is abundant with these kinds of blessings.

If you were abused as a child, it makes great sense that you have gone through life on your own, emotionally; that you have kept a part of yourself very protected. There is a room that is a part of you to which the door has been closed. You may not even know what is in that room; most likely you do not. The old trunk in the attic may hold treasures, perhaps musty, but we do not see them until it is opened and the pieces are held to the light.

You probably would not want to open that door to anyone. Being open makes you feel afraid that you will be abused or abandoned again. You may be unaware of the beliefs and expectations you have about this. Most likely you are not aware of these because they were put away in the room along with fear and hurt and mistrust.

Having healthy relationships may seem like a mystery or an overwhelming task or just impossible. The healthy, curious child you once were may have been put away in that room, too, so she is unavailable to feel and assert her way to being close to others. But you are in charge of finding the missing pieces of yourself and holding them to the light. Your process must be slow enough for you to feel safe.

Growing in Safety

Meditation: Creating Your Safe Place

Relax quietly and soften your surroundings as well as yourself with warmth: sun, music, peacefulness. Begin with the "Loosening" meditation. Then imagine being anywhere you want that is beautiful and peaceful. Create a "safety zone" surrounding you and protecting you from harm. Envision a strong, bright light that reflects negativity away but mixes and radiates with kindness.

You can find a safe place within you; there, you are loving, gentle, and calm. As you learn to trust in your ability to create this environment for yourself, you will begin to learn what you need to do to be safe both inside and out.

Describe your safe place. Go there in your mind. Encircle yourself with white light.

Meditation: The Way to Inner Knowing

Inner knowing comes from a voice inside you that may be very quiet if it has been silenced by abuse or repression. To connect with it will be like exercising newly-found muscles: the more you listen, the louder it will become.

Be in a quiet place and breathe deeply. Relax fully and focus your attention at the center of your chest while doing this meditation.

Where is your inner voice? How and where do you "know" something? When you feel good "vibes" or bad ones, from where in your body do these feelings emanate?

Try out your ability to know something from within: take an example of a choice or decision you are trying to make. Gently envision (or write) your two or three options. Without debating or reasoning, simply focus on each and detect whether you have a "go ahead" feeling, a confused feeling, or a "stop sign." Clear yourself by breathing and relaxing, and try the same exercise several times.

If you have trouble with this, try "tuning in" to something you feel positive about and see where and how this feels in your body; then do the same with something about which you feel negative. When you can do this, try again on the earlier part of this exercise that involves making a choice or decision.

You can have a stronger and stronger connection with your inner knowing. This will help you be more safe and more successful with your life.

Practice: Believing is Succeeding

Allowing yourself to believe you are not a victim of outside or inside influences allows you to become who you truly are.

Imagine trying a new activity, class, or sport believing you will fail. Then notice how you feel if you believe you will succeed. Do you have more energy? More enjoyment? Note experiences you have had when you believed you would succeed or fail, and note the outcome:

If you believe you will succeed, your chances of doing so are noticeably greater than if you envision failure. Belief is one way you can create control in your life.

List some specific beliefs about yourself you can change to receive the kind of treatment you want from others:

You can choose what you believe. And your beliefs can change your life.

Meditation: Growing Beautiful

Once you have begun to heal, you may be able to open up to positive feelings you had before you were abused. Focus your state of relaxation on this suggestion and then do the following exercise.

Picture yourself as a child. See yourself as you looked then, as you were dressed, doing something you liked to do. Remember good feelings and fun events. Find at least one positive memory. (If you think this is not possible, work at it until you do.)

Imagine growing forward from then. Let the child of that time grow into an adult and picture the beauty of growing like a tree forming and reaching to the sky, surrounding its scars with burls. Woodcarvers say the burls are the most beautiful pieces from which to create.

Sit on the floor and imagine yourself as a tree starting to grow taller and reach out to the light. Raise yourself, stretch your arms, enjoy the burls you grow beyond.

Practice: Image Your Healing

One way to heal is to bathe negative images in favorite images. A client of mine realized that she felt like a sow bug rolled up into a protective ball. To change this defensive feeling, she imagined herself in a favorite yoga leg stretch and as she opened and expanded from being curled up, she infused the image of herself with bright, coral light.

There was a tall church spire visible outside my office window. It reminded one client of the painful penetration she experienced as a toddler when her father violently abused her. She was very disturbed by it. Together we began revisualizing the spire softening into bright yellow-white light. Whenever any feeling of trauma began to emerge as she saw or thought of the spire, she created this visual transformation and was never again overwhelmed by the traumatic association.

Take a negative image, something you fear or dislike. Change its size to smaller or its color to one you like. Watch as you can transform it into something different that is not negative. Make notes below of your imaging process.

Practice: Playing Yourself—You are One of a Kind

You are like a musical instrument. You can learn to play yourself. Your style, your pitch, your resonance will be different from anyone else's.

What instrument are you? Describe why.

Meditation: Getting to Know Heart

To relate to others from your heart does not mean to give your heart away. You may live from your heart without allowing it to be invaded.

Relax quietly and soften your surroundings as well as yourself with warmth: sun, music, peacefulness. Use this suggestion to the extent that it feels possible and good for you.

Draw yourself with soft, pink-colored banners going out to someone you care for. Label the banners with positive feelings. Stay in your stance of directing these feelings out. Feel your strength. If you can do this easily, try maintaining comfort while allowing one of these banners to return and embrace you.

Practice: Allowing Yourself to Receive

Therapy is different from other social contexts in that it is solely for you. If you are in therapy, you are not there to meet your therapist's needs. Letting yourself receive in this way can correct for when you have been wrongfully used by someone else to meet their needs.

When have you let someone be there just for you?

Who could you ask for this now?

A Closing Contemplation: Nourishing Waves

You may want to use this image many times over for support and emotional nourishment. Meditation and prayer can be like a constant song. Through them you can build connection with your spiritual self. Being one link in the chain of life means you are never alone in spirit.

As you let yourself experience this, imagine yourself swelling like the waves of the ocean, carrying your energy forth, bubbling, splashing, moving, breathing, to fold again into your self. This is the nourishing of your soul.

Opening

Practice: Finding Your Smile

Providing for all dimensions of self-care includes the physical, the emotional, and the spiritual. If you have not experienced the spiritual, let yourself see the wonder of nature. There is purpose to everything. Solutions are provided to every problem.

How do you feel outdoors; in woods, fields, mountains? On a sunny day? On a rainy day? What animals do you see and enjoy? How do you feel in the country as compared to the city? Do you see things, animals, plants, life, as connected? What is your favorite place? Why?

Practice: Spiritual Help

Spiritual help will come when invited. Good spiritual energy will not intrude on your process, and you will feel uplifted by it. Negative spiritual energy is intimidating or controlling, and you might know it by feeling afraid to trust in yourself.

Your spiritual self knows what you need. A voice in your chest will say, "This is right for me." It is like being at a traffic light that turns green and a small feeling inside says, "Go ahead now."

How can you seek spiritual help? Can you detect experiences that create a "green-light" feeling in you? When are you open or receptive? If you pray, do you listen?.

Practice: Trusting Your Intuition

Freedom will be found by opening to healing energy. Open yourself to your intuition and your spiritual self. You will be led to experiences that will help you heal.

Recall a time when you "followed your gut" and pursued a plan based upon trust in yourself. How did it turn out? Now recall a time when you trusted someone else's opinion of what you should do. How would you compare the feelings?

Practice: Your Body Is Yours

You are the source of your sensuality. Your feelings originate in you. In healing, try to imagine how slowly a child might grow naturally into her body feelings. Allow yourself the same gentle pace now because you are nurturing that child into adulthood. If you were sexually abused and feel your body betrayed you, if you feel hatred toward your body, remember your body is also that which is allowing you to have this experience of living.

Note three or more sensations in your body that you enjoy. Examples: a yawn; hanging your feet in a stream; or hitting the ball with the "sweet spot" of your tennis racquet.

Practice: Healing from Memories

Remembering bad things that happened to you and how you felt about them makes them real again. You can use this to heal by seeing back to who you were and feeling the difference between then and now. You can see your new self in beauty and strength.

Allow yourself a familiar neutral or positive memory from your childhood. Note ways you are stronger or smarter now.

The very same growth has happened since you last had a bad experience.

A Meditation on Opening: Quenching Your Thirst, Filling the Void

At times we fear opening because we fear experiencing a void within ourselves. This feeling of emptiness can be transformed whenever we pause to drink from life.

Close your eyes and relax. Recall a sound of a waterfall tumbling into a clear, beautiful pond. Take your thirst to this place. Visualize yourself standing expectantly, reaching with open arms and raising your mouth to drink in abundance. Let the falls quench your thirst as well as your need to be refreshed.

Do this exercize slowly and end with a bow of thanks.

The gesture of drinking keeps abundance flowing.

Action

Practice: Self-Disclosure

Sharing your feelings and some of your story with others who have been or are being abused is sharing healing. It may prevent further abuse of others.

Is there someone to whom you feel ready to tell any part of your story? Write down any possibilities.

Practice: Public Action/Personal Release

You may choose public action as one way to resolve your experience. If you do this, let it be a way of releasing negative energy. Let the record book of the universe hold others accountable so that you are free to let yourself go on to build a new life. If you use the legal system, do it with this in mind.

Practice letting go of negative thoughts: think of something you feel tense or anxious about. Collect these feelings in your gut, encircle them in your mind with silk, imagine sliding them down a slippery chute to rest away from you. You may also think of something you worry about. Form the worry in your mind and place it in a cloud and watch it float away.

If you choose public action, protect yourself from negative involvement. Use these techniques to release your feelings.

Practice: Parenting Yourself

Self-care is often very difficult. We are surrounded by the temptations of technology: junk food, drugs, television, possessions, busyness. More and more we are seduced into seeking satisfaction outside ourselves. If you have been abused, you learned not to access your inner self because of the pain there. Finding love for yourself will gradually change your tendency to disregard your body's need for care, nutrition, and movement. Set goals that provide for your body's health, and lovingly take your self in hand to change bad habits. Begin with small, simple changes in order to establish trust in yourself that your habits *can be* changed.

An example of this process may be helpful.

1. Habit change I desire:	*Watch less television*
2. Concrete goal:	*Watch up to two hours per day*
List positive motivators:	***(a)** "I'll have time to find out who I am and what I like or what I want to do."*
	***(b)** "I'll eat fewer snack foods because I tend to snack when I watch television."*
List feelings of resistance:	***(a)** "I'm afraid that I can't find anything else to do."*
	***(b)** "I feel less lonely watching television."*
Respond to resistance:	***(a)** "I won't have a chance to find anything else to do if I watch television too much."*
	***(b)** "I won't solve my problem of loneliness if I watch so much television."*
3. Establish a plan:	*Write a tentative schedule for television viewing*

4. Start the plan and give yourself positive reinforcement (your own personal cheering squad), either in the form of gold stars, feeling good, or a new activity you enjoy.

Make your own outline using a habit change you want to make.

Habit Change Outline

1. Habit

2. Goal

   Positive Motivators (Rewards)

   Resistance

   Response (Restart) to Resistance

3. Plan

4. Reward I Will Give Myself

Practice: Welcoming Your Personal Support Squad

Some of the hardest habits to change are self-destructive ones that arose out of previous pain. At the time, they were the best options you had to meet needs for comfort, escape, nurturance, and love. They can be replaced by inner calm, inner acceptance, self-care, and loving kindness. When you experience even one new moment of peace, let yourself feel gratitude and reward. As you enrich your experience this way, your inner calm will be reproduced ten-fold.

Picture an inner support squad with looks on their faces of hope, pleasure, and support. These might be friends you have had or hoped for. Perhaps an old childhood buddy. Or your imaginary idea of what a best friend would be like. Maybe you visualize a team like the Seven Dwarfs with names you choose (like "Calm," "Caring," "Joy," "Peaceful," "Fun-loving"). Or perhaps they wear uniforms and cheer each time you need encouragement. Describe your squad. How do you want them to support you? How do they do this? List one sign that lets you know your squad is present.

Practice: There Is a Larger Giver of Life Than You

You may worry about being selfish when you have an opportunity to take care of yourself. The belief that meeting another's needs must be at your own expense is false.

Do you feel guilty doing things for yourself? Whose needs were you asked and taught to meet when you were growing up? Write these names down. What needs of theirs are you really responsible for now?

Practice: Reruns for Change—Getting Respect

If you desire change in the way someone else is treating you, quietly focus on the respectful attitude with which you would like to be treated. When you experience the situation again, return your focus to the kindness you would like. By changing your focus of attention in this way, you encourage the opening for change.

Imagine a casual acquaintance who is doing something to you that is irritating you. Create positive thoughts about that person: positive qualities you can see, or just your desire to develop good will. Enjoy the goodness you feel. Note how this changes your behavior from previous times. And how you can ask for what you want. Experiment with a friend.

Practice: Master of Yourself

You may feel your sexuality has been taken from you if you have been sexually abused. If so, you can reclaim your feelings, your self as your source, your needs, your rights, including the right to say no or to change your mind.

In the next week, identify something you committed yourself to that you do not want to do. Respectfully tell another person that you changed your mind about your commitment. Make notes to yourself about times you have over-committed yourself in the past. Note how you could have prevented this from happening.

Now imagine yourself in a situation that is sexual in nature. To grow stronger in your knowledge that you have the freedom to make choices, create some phrases that are personally comfortable to describe different choices. Examples may be: "I'd like to wait longer before I do that," "I need to go slower," or "I'd like to take the lead."

Practice: The Power of Expectation

If you test your partner or a friend to see if they can fill your empty space, they will fail because you are already filling it with mistrust.

What examples do you have of when you expect nothing and get nothing? What about when you expect something positive and have a good experience?

Practice: The Zen of Interaction

If you feel guilty for your needs, guilty for your wants, guilty because you want to have that which you believe you do not deserve, practice the act of receiving or accepting.

Connect to your graciousness by passing an object back and forth between you and a friend. First, take it from each other. Then push it at each other. Then receive it with open, caring hands. Then give it with warmth and generosity.

Describe how you felt.

Practice: Untether Yourself

You may feel angry that God has not protected you from being abused. This is anger about your vulnerability, your feelings of weakness, your powerlessness at the time. This is part of the human condition. If you were not human you would not be having feelings. One way not to feel trapped by the human experience is to discover the feelings you like having. You can exercise your free will in this way.

Think of a feeling you like having, even if it is something as simple as the lightheartedness or comfort of a bubble bath. Make a list of several feelings you like to have, and next to one, an activity that creates the feeling, for example:

feel calm........................light a candle

feel healthy....................play softball

Now either do or make a plan to do something you would like, considering the feeling you need in your life at this time.

A Closing Meditation: About Action

Consider that life is to be managed rather than overcome.

If you like, refer to this idea many times over as you use this book.

Pursuing Change

Practice: Flowing

By changing, you break the connection and the power others have held over you

Envision a solid bridge of connection between you and your self, and let the rivers of grief and loss flow under the bridge.

Draw a picture of this and label rivulets with memories you wish to put behind you.

When you are finished, be thankful for rivers.

Practice: Strength Is in the Positive

If you needed to be strong to endure pain and fear in the past, that is one thing. But do not be misled into thinking you need to feel pain and fear in the present in order to feel powerful. This would be a waste of the present.

Note times you feel strong when there is no threat. Are you alone, or with others? Are you happy? Carefully contemplate what makes you feel happy and strong at the same time.

Practice: On Power; The Lesson of the Feather

A client of mine who was abused by her father was terrified by the snake lurking in her inner-imagined forest, encroaching on her enjoyment of the beauty she saw around her. Over the course of some weeks, she began putting form to her fear by changing the forest to a place she loved: a swimming pool. She envisioned the snake swimming threateningly and she also began seeing some different kinds of small fish. Groups of fish that characterized different feelings began gathering. At the same time, she found she could lock the snake in a cage in the corner of the pool. After feeling powerful in overcoming her fear, she unlocked the cage. As she returned to the forest, she could imagine the snake as her father. She propped him in the palm of her hand like a feather and blew him away.

Try changing the image of a bad memory. Imagine a place where you are safe and comfortable and begin casting the person you fear in different roles. Make yourself larger or more powerful than that person.

Practice: Weaving Life from Grief

Watch your grief. You may use it to moderate the speed at which you are changing. You may rediscover it when new losses occur, and when new gains are made. Picture grief as the weft of your fabric and life as the warp. The deeper the weft is, the higher the weave will be. Depth and complexity can make for a rich life.

Draw a colored, plaid pattern of how your life used to be. Then begin adding lines and colors that represent new themes or feelings in your life.

Practice: Standing with Your Truth—"Accepting" Your Past

You may have been told that acceptance of your history is vital to recovery. You may reject this notion because it sounds like you would be condoning the abuse you have experienced. Think of acceptance as an acknowledgement. To *acknowledge* is to know your reality; it is simply to see it.

Put your hands out in front of you, palms up, and place your history in your hands. Look directly at your past and see it without trying to change it or do anything about it. This holding is all you have to do to begin accepting the fact of the abuse.

Practice: Airing Out Your Truth—Caring for Your Past

Acceptance of what happened to you means being honest with yourself. It does not mean you chose what happened or would allow it now. Acceptance means acknowledgement, and this allows you to take care of your pain.

Think of a child with a scraped knee. To heal, the knee needs cleansing and a bandage, then air. All of our wounds need this care. Write about a wound of yours and what it would mean to cleanse, bandage, and air it.

Practice: You Have the Right to Your Expectations

If you hope that someone who hurt you may acknowledge what they did, you will have healthy expectations. You have the right to expect someone who hurt you to be sorry. Do not back down from your expectations even if they are not met.

If you do not receive what you think you deserve, it may mean the person cannot be trusted. But you still deserve compassion. What did you want from him or her? Can you give this to yourself? How?

Practice: Apologies Are a Beginning

If someone apologizes, it does not mean you have to forgive. Their apology is the opening to whether or not a relationship proceeds.

Think of someone you would not want to have a relationship with even if they apologize for something that hurt you. Why?

Practice: Transforming Guilt

Healing always includes acceptance (acknowledgement) and forgiveness. With acceptance you open your consciousness to truth. With self-forgiveness you open your heart to yourself, others, and your spiritual self. Forgiving yourself releases the hold the past has on you. It is human and normal to feel guilty.

Write something you are guilty of, and what you want to do about it. For example, write "I was rude in what I said to Katherine." Record options in response, such as apologizing to Katherine, avoiding Katherine, or continuing to feel guilty. Note the positive feelings an apology can bring you. This is a respectful way of forgiving yourself. You are honoring Katherine as well as honoring your humanness.

Practice: Trust Honesty

If a person who hurt you does not remember or will not remember, you can hold them accountable for forgetting. Stand in your own reality; a relationship cannot grow forward without the trust that comes from honesty.

Was the person who abused you alcoholic or otherwise impaired? If so, this is one reason you deserve help in healing. The abuser may not be available to work things through with you. Write your own conversation, imagining you are talking to him or her.

Practice: Developing the Skill of Reliance

We do not *have* to struggle. We need to take care of our business: the daily tasks, the maintenance, the joy, the pursuit of work and pleasure and loving. These are the reins we are in charge of, but to keep life from feeling like a battle, let your spiritual self seek help.

From what sources outside yourself can you seek help? (Remember both practical and spiritual help.)

A Closing Meditation: Pursuing Change

There are things we cannot change. If we think of life as being like a deck of cards, we cannot change the hand we were dealt, but we can learn the art of the game.

If you like, refer to this idea many times over as you use this book.

CHAPTER SIX

A COURSE OF HEALING

THE LIFE OF FEELINGS

This chapter is about healing through feeling. When bad things happen, it is the beauty of our human nature that we are given tools to cope. Anxiety, denial, dissociation, and even depression, are gifts for survival. After they have done the job of protecting, however, these coping skills leave a residue. One of the thickest layers of residue is that feelings of all kinds are fought and feared rather than accepted and felt. You have needed to protect yourself from your feelings when you were being abused. Because of the "overwhelm," betrayal, intimidation, and perhaps physical pain you experienced, you needed to absent your feeling self in order to survive. The feelings you had were normal and healthy, but the situation was not.

Anyone who has not experienced trauma and the process of regrowing may not appreciate the difficulty of opening the doors again to feeling. It is resisted at every level because the original association of needing protection from feelings was planted when survival (physical, emotional, spiritual, and psychological) was very much at risk. There may even have been planted an inner struggle of control, a determination not to feel, lest the abuser win in the struggle of wills that was left after physical control was achieved.

We have described a process of intimidation which leaves victims vulnerable to depression, shame, rage, isolation, and behaviors motivated by defensiveness. The path of healing requires a journey back to the inner self. Every feeling is like a pebble lining the path back to the self. It is crucial that the pebbles on this path be seen, felt, valued, and sought out, because this is, in itself, the path of life.

You have made your way to this point in this book, learning about abuse as well as your defenses against it. We have shared meditations—gentle help for you to know your inner resources better. You may have determined some things you need help with from other people. Perhaps your life is already looking different to you.

Please do not hurry your work or rush your feelings. Also, please have sources of emotional and physical support available so that, if feelings get rocky, you will find calm. Take your work at a comfortable pace—now is not the time to force the process. Feelings can at times seem overwhelming and you are in the process of building your capabilities. Compare what you know about yourself now to what you knew when you began this book.

We invite you to gather your learning and your strength to explore the life of feelings and the feelings that make up life.

Having Feelings

Meditation: Comfort Alone

Relax quietly and soften your surroundings as well as yourself with warmth: sun, music, peacefulness. Use this suggestion to the extent that it feels possible and good for you.

Though you may feel lonely, you are never really alone. Listen for the still, small, kind voice within you and let it radiate as far as you can imagine. Then listen carefully for its resonance.

Imagine your existence like a pebble thrown in a pool of water, radiating in ever-widening circles. Then imagine you are the pool, providing a space for your soul's reverberations.

Practice: Your Differentness

If you have been abused, you may feel shame in your differentness. You *are* different from other people. You have individual feelings, opinions, and interests. Let your differentness validate you.

List some qualities that are particular to you. Rule out any that you feel are positive or negative. List at least three that carry no judgment.

Your issues and feelings deserve as much attention as anyone else's. Otherwise, why would you exist?

Practice: Closeness—Not Sameness

In seeking closeness with another, if you are wanting them to feel the same feeling you do, you may be doing so to validate yourself or to feel that they care for you. This may keep you from receiving the caring that is there.

Cite times you wanted someone else to feel the same way you did about someone or something. Why did you want them to feel the same way?

Practice: Dealing with Pain

Emotional pain is akin to physical pain. It is our soul's way of signaling that we need comfort, care, security, and healing.

Think of a time when you were alone and in emotional pain. Note this.

Now think of a time you were in pain but had comfort from someone else or within yourself.

List resources for help when you are in emotional pain. (More than one)

Practice: Cultivating Resources for Living

If you feel that dying would be better than feeling your pain, your shame, or your depression, seek help in changing. Getting help will break your task into more manageable pieces.

Make a list of new sources of help you want to pursue. Set goals for pursuing one at a time.

Example:	***Goal***	***Steps***
	join a support group	*make 3 phone calls in the next week to locate one*

Practice: You Are as Real as Everyone Else

The validity of your feelings is not up for debate. No one but you can deny your reality.

A great deal of anguish is caused when we put energy into trying to convince someone to validate or accept our feelings. Name some things you feel that are not up to anyone else to determine or judge.

Practice: Cradling Your Feelings

If you feel overwhelmed or feel you need help handling feelings, hold them to your heart; rock them like an infant; surround them with protective energy. You will not die from having feelings. You will wither only by putting your life-sustaining energy to use in trying to bury feelings.

Imagine a recent event and rock your feelings in your arms. Note images that come to mind.

Practice: Balancing Joy with Pain

Your pain is proof of how sensitive you are. You can feel joy only to the degree that you feel pain. Life comes furnished with balance.

Our capacity for feeling includes both pain and joy. The path of your pain may have become deeply trodden, and it requires determination to forge a new route on the path to joy. One way this can be done is by creating the idea of joy and reinforcing it. In your mind's eye, this can create new receptivity and ease of access to any feeling.

Name one activity or situation in which you feel joy. Practice thinking about this for the sole purpose of feeling joy. Deepen the path of your joy.

Practice: Finding Stillness

When you were hurt you experienced some kind of pain. To keep yourself from feeling more pain, you may have kept yourself from experiencing many feelings. You may believe everything will be painful, everyone will hurt you eventually. To come alive, you must be with yourself peacefully, allowing feelings to move through you without trying to get away from them. With stillness, feelings will naturally arise in layers, allowing you to address them gradually. In the meantime, notice when you feel bored, comfortable, neutral, or just okay. Find and nourish yourself with these times. Stillness can be safe.

Describe some of the still moments you find.

Managing Feelings

Learning to handle feelings is like starting to work out at a gym: you need to develop new muscle groups. Feelings are like muscles: the more they are exercised, the stronger you become. You can always value them this way.

Practice: You Are More Than Your Feelings

When you feel strong emotions and begin to be overwhelmed or managed by them, you may experience fear and then tension. When you feel overwhelmed by emotion, train yourself to relax and drain the energy away by visualizing a sieve, or a system of underground rivers, or a red ball dissipating into blue shooting stars. If you take a few deep breaths and image your relaxation, you will begin to learn being in charge of your emotions, and unpleasantness will pass.

Imagine a situation that brings up a strong feeling for you, such as anger or fear. Apply one of these images, for example: put anger in a red ball in front of you; make it redder and redder; then take some deep breaths as you let the red go in many directions. As it disperses, let it be cooled and changed to blue. See if you can relax so much that your relaxation is greater than your anger. This is what is meant by "letting go." You feel your feelings and you identify what it is and what it is about. You then make it so much smaller than who you are that you can decide what to do about the situation that created it.

Write down the feeling you chose and the image you used to make it bigger, to release it, and to make it smaller. Imagine using this technique with a number of feelings.

Practice: Greeting Your Needs

Feeling is different from acting. Give yourself permission not to have to do anything with your feelings. Try not to choose them. You *can* choose behaviors.

Note feelings you have and a positive behavior to go along with each. For example, feeling irritable may signal you to listen to a relaxation tape;

feeling angry, you may choose to go for a walk; feeling sad, you may play the piano.

Feeling	*Behavior*

Practice: Embracing Your Needs Instead of Being Shamed

If needs feel shameful, it is not because needs are shameful. It is because your needs were not considered or valued when you were a child. When childhood needs are "left hanging," the child feels like she is left hanging, and shame comes in to fill the void. You can fill this void with care and loving kindness.

Note something you are ashamed of (like going places alone, tripping on the sidewalk, etc.). Imagine this in a child. Now notice how you feel toward that child.

Once your heart is in gear, you can always replace shame with compassion.

Practice: The Puppy Exercise

Feel the difference between compassion and self-pity. Picture a puppy, innocence, or yourself as a child. Compassion feels open and free. Self-pity feels closed and tight. If you find yourself wanting people to feel sorry for you, it is because you are needing compassion from yourself and others.

Look at the toddler again. Close your eyes and imagine a puppy tired out from a walk, and then picture yourself as a child, sleepy and tearful. Sense the feelings you have toward the puppy, the feeling perhaps of affection and sympathy. Nuzzle or hold the puppy. Now in your mind replace the puppy with your tired child self and comfort her. Describe how it feels to have compassion instead of pity.

Practice: Whisking Away Pretense

Because you have had to deny yourself feelings when you were being abused, you may have learned to say, "I'm fine," "I'm happy," "Everything's okay," "I can take care of myself." Pretending prevents you from knowing yourself and your needs. If you have been pretending, use your awareness to tune into your true feelings. You will gain the power that comes from acknowledgement.

Your power lies in the truth of your feeling, not in the kind of feeling. Note times you were pretending: pretending to feel happy when you were not, agreeable when you were not, etc. Note what you really felt. Note times when you really felt happy.

You do not need to *do* anything with this information.

Practice: Safe Vision for Remembering

You must have protection from the hurt and stress of bad memories. Bringing spiritual power from within yourself can provide this safety.

Find a peaceful place to be and consider doing this exercise with a friend nearby. Breathe deeply and, as you feel calm, imagine yourself surrounded by bright white light. Recast your mind several times to strengthening this hoop around you.

Now think of a familiar bad memory. See this clearly in your mind's eye. Surround the memory with a second hoop of bright white light. You can now view your memory from the safety of the present moment..

How does it help to image yourself as separate from the memory?

Practice: Speaking Your Spirituality

What are your spiritual beliefs? Is this present life all there is? Is there a power greater than human? If you believe there is, what do you call it? Do you believe you can call on it for help? If you believe there is nothing to the universe but this life, what is the purpose of being here? If you believe there is no greater source of help than human, you may feel perpetually lonely or depressed. Take these questions and see if you can describe your purpose in being here. From where does life energy come? What would you call this energy?

Some people believe that our sole purpose is to find joy.

Practice: Standing in Your Fear

Fear can be:

a signal of danger
an impediment to growth
a helpful reminder of the past
your enemy
your friend

Using the above list, note examples of when fear can show itself to you in these ways.

Stand in your fear with both feet. Ask for spiritual help. Do everything you can to protect yourself and have faith.

Moving Through Feelings

Emotions require energy. Our different kinds of feelings require and give back different kinds of energy. Humor and joy, for example, make us more lively as well as healthier. One reason the work of dealing with feelings is important is to free up negative energy for other aspects of life. These aspects have feelings attached to them but are not bound up by them. For example, we cannot do our work well if we are weighted down by depression. Or we have no motivation to go biking if we are too worried about being alone. When we move through feelings to set our mind on a goal, we can reap the satisfactions that come from attaining that goal or doing an activity. This gives us new energy again and again. Renewal is part of the natural cycle of life. You can learn to expect it.

Practice: Unraveling Anger

Anger must be unraveled knot by knot, like making use out of a knotted ball of twine. If too much force is used, the problem is only made worse. With the intent and meditation of an artist, pieces of anger must be touched gently.

Take a tangled ball of twine and unravel it gently. Imagine each knot as the tension you feel when angry. Use gentle gestures to loosen the twine. Think of this as relaxation of your anger. Do this for fifteen minutes. (If you do not have twine, use a messy pile of sewing thread, a tangled garden hose, or do something else that requires patience to untangle.)

Practice: Holding Anger

You may feel angry and outraged. If you discover these feelings, hold them with great care. Wait until your anger informs you of your needs before you go to someone with it.

Identify your anger about something. Hold these feelings gently. What do they tell you about your needs? Consider a number of possible needs. When your anger subsides is the best time to express the need. Make notes until you arrive at what you want to ask for.

Practice: The Soul of Grief

It is necessary to feel grief in order to move through it. Grief is life, grief is growth, grief cultivates the fields of our soul and allows us also to feel love and joy.

Recall a time you are aware of when you felt grief. Describe as well as you can what you first felt and the feelings that followed.

Did you mention that the grief did lessen?

Practice: The Birthing Canal of Grief

Grief can be a birthing canal. But you have to stay in it and trust in nature taking its course.

Identify a loss: something or someone who has left you or has changed or died. Do you have tears or a heavy feeling in your chest? Do you have a tight throat? Do you blame someone for your pain? These are all descriptions of grief. How do you feel grief? Notice that it comes in cycles and that, with time, it diminishes.

Practice: Follow Your Grief to Where It Leads You

If you feel like your grief about a particular event will never end, you may not have embraced it fully. Have faith that when you do embrace it you will also be able to release it.

Who or what is this grief about?

Was there another loss before this that was similar?

Another since?

Is there a common theme to losses you have experienced?

Focus again on the grief you feel will never end. What is a larger meaning of this loss to you?

*Are you responsible for the loss in any way? Are you in **grief** or **guilt?***

A client I worked with was in a perpetual state of grief over the loss of a child given up for adoption. When she acknowledged that she had made the choice for many reasons, and understood that she was not equipped to take responsibility for the child, her grief was alleviated. She could let go of the grief by feeling her guilt and taking responsibility for choosing.

Practice: The Curative Power of Sadness

Sadness connected to love is redeemed by the love. Sadness connected to anger is never redeemed. Feelings fueled by anger do not help you heal.

Can you identify examples of this in your own life? Note times of sadness connected with love.

Now note losses you have experienced about which you are angry. Consider what sadness you may have.

Practice: The Bath Sponge and Sexual Feelings

You may have many negative associations with sexual feelings of which you are both aware and unaware. Because of this, you may become anxious if you experience sexual arousal. Before trying to experience positive sexual feelings with another person, you may be well served by exploring the feelings alone first. Use the analogy of the bath sponge to ease yourself into these feelings.

If sexual feelings are frightening for you, imagine yourself as a soft bath sponge that can slowly and gently expand and absorb water. Let the water represent sexual feeling. Your sexual feelings will not overwhelm you once you allow them to breathe.

Name sensations you like and can absorb.

Practice: A Visit from Happiness

Happiness can be frightening because in the past it has been elusive and without permanence. You can change this in the present by welcoming happiness as a visitor. Be assured it will return if invited.

Think of the most recent time you felt content, even if just for a moment. What are some words that describe that moment? If you can recapture this feeling, can you imagine having a sense of gratitude for it? Work at adding to this by making a list of happy moments.

Practice: Forgiveness Is Yours

If you decide it is beneficial for you to forgive someone who hurt you, know that to have spiritual compassion for someone is a different matter from having a relationship with that person, or condoning what they did.

Name someone you have forgiven for something but do not want to have a friendship with.

If friendship was required of forgiveness, we could not forgive those who have died.

Practice: A Heart Exercise

Be led by your heart. It will never let you down.

Can you feel warmth in your heart? Imagine your heart being open, then feel it hard, cold, closed. An open heart leads you to connection with others.

Using the space below, use crayons to draw two hearts, one open and one closed. Note the colors you chose to make the heart feel open and those you chose which make it feel closed.

The more you are able to open and close your heart, the more choice you will have for love.

Practice: Your Summary

Use this space to summarize your reactions if you have learned anything new about your feelings. Are certain feelings easier than others for you either to have or identify? With which feelings do you have the most experience? With which are you least familiar? With whom can you talk about feelings?

CHAPTER SEVEN

WALKING THE PATH OF CHANGE TOGETHER

If you have been there, you know some of how abuse looks, acts, and feels. Perhaps you found yourself identifying with things we referred to in *The Eye of the Storm*. You have also had the opportunity to explore for yourself how you came to be in an abusive relationship. We have looked at origins of this in your family history. If there are further pieces of this you want to put together, if you are confused about how it all fits, use this book in conjunction with a domestic violence group, a therapist, or call the National Domestic Violence Hotline at 1-800-799-SAFE.

If you are ready to proceed, perhaps you have already extricated yourself from a violent relationship. You may be wanting to build a new relationship that is healthier and safe. Or you may be reading this as a couple, wanting to initiate change in your current relationship. Two actions on your part will go a long way to ensuring your success:

Number One: If your relationship is currently physically abusive, you must *establish safety for each of you.*

If you are being hurt, you must have the safety of distance and/or the protection of friends or relatives. If you are hurting your partner and are so emotionally involved that you do not think you could physically separate, that is, you don't think you could stay away, you need to know that you, too, are in danger. You are not in control, and you must acknowledge that you cannot maintain control yet if you are with your partner. When you have worked on your own issues you may be able to live together again. If you need to separate, getting help will greatly increase your chances of success. Find and attend a treatment group for men or partners who are dealing with violent behavior. Taking responsibility this way can be an instant source of pride for you and will help you get moving.

Number Two: The second action you can take to ensure success is to sign on. By this we mean commit, to yourself and your partner, that you want to end abuse in your relationship.

You may know the relationship cannot continue if violence does, but at this point do not take on the greater issue of whether or not your relationship will endure. Focus solely on ending the violence or emotional abuse. The future of your relationship will take care of itself.

We begin couples work with exercises to help you understand both roles that are necessary to an abusive relationship: the victim, or "Underdog," and the abuser, or "Dominator." It is not always the case that these roles stay constant. Victims do not just "take it." If you are abusing someone, you are getting back, in some form, what you are putting out. If you are to work as a couple, your commitment must be to ending abuse, any part in it you have, rather than focusing on just one partner. If one of you, though, becomes truly out of tune with destructiveness, the abuse *will* end—either the abusing partner will change or the relationship will end.

Who You Are in Your Relationship

If you have been physically or sexually abused, the self you have created to cope with life is likely to be highly skillful and intelligent. You have created some niche, some identity, some sources of comfort, and perhaps even worldly success. Even if you experience on-going depression, phobias, or panic attacks, you probably experience some of the blessings of life such as home, friends, family, physical health, and enjoyable activities.

Whether you feel like you are barely managing to stay alive or your life feels full of amenities, you have inside you the spiritual self that was terribly hurt. Your inner experience is connected to having been abused. It may not be until you go deeply inside yourself that you will discover the fear, the need to control, the pain that resides as a part of your experience of life and others. Or it may be that these aspects of your inner self are all too familiar to you.

You have had to live your life with a great deal of attention to protection rather than freedom. It would be impossible for you to be talked out of your need for protection—which is as it should be. But you may be overlooking the realm of life that flows like a spring or a fountain, is peaceful like a meadow, that holds you in spiritual confidence. Life provides allure for you to experience warmth, joy, power, and spontaneity. These experiences will be your invitation to choose to live in a new dimension and to live connected to your heart.

Practice: Living is Deserving

If you find that your identity is built around having been abused, find out what you would lose or give up if you changed this belief. You will be able to find a healthy replacement for the loss. A client of mine believed that, as a victim, she had validity. If she was not a victim, she did not deserve to have her feelings. You would not be alive if you were not deserving.

Imagine some things you know you deserve, like having a place to live or being able to sleep. You deserve those simply because you are alive. List some additional things you deserve.

Practice: Directing Your Feelings

When you are in your victim self, you believe you are controlled by your feelings or by other people. One alternative is for you to choose how you want to direct your feelings. You can establish guidelines for how you want to express a feeling and for how long. For example, you may decide to express anger by yelling into a pillow for sixty seconds. Tune into how much time and energy you want to use in any given way.

Chart this, for example:

Feeling	***Activity***	***Time***
anger	*write about my anger*	*1 hour per day*
joy	*playing with my dog*	*double what I currently do*
anxiety	*meditate or listen to relaxing music*	*twenty minutes*

Practice: Changing Feelings—From Powerlessness to Control

If you have been with an abusive partner, you have probably felt powerless. You may have experienced this as anger, hopelessness, depression, or anxiety. You may have expressed it by pouting, keeping secrets, manipulating, seducing, being angry a lot, or even by becoming passive.

In other words, your feeling powerless has caused some behaviors by you; defenses that do not further you, enhance you, or express who you are. This pattern causes a vicious cycle as you feel increasingly controlled and resentful. Beginning to claim control within yourself will help you reclaim your life.

Changing feelings can change your life.

List times you recall feeling powerless with your partner. What are ways that you reacted? Take a few examples and identify how you could deal directly with your partner, for example, by making a statement or request.

You may not get what you ask for but how your partner responds either builds your trust and good feeling or undermines it. And whether or not you are satisfied, you have saved a lot of energy you would have used in defenses.

Practice: Beginning Self-Protection

Trust: Do not trust anyone who is abusing you. You may love him, or feel you need her to support you, but do not trust them. Put your trust in yourself, in friends, and in your spiritual connection until your partner proves he or she has learned new behavior.

List new behaviors you have learned for protection.

Practice: Effective Vigilance

Being in your victim-self sometimes means thinking you need to protect yourself when there is no threat, or not protecting yourself when danger is a reality. You may imagine a threat when there is none or ignore real danger.

List times and places when you could be in real danger. Note at least two times and places when you are physically safe.

Practice: Don't Be Fooled—The Sliding Glass Door

You must avail yourself of all resources for self-protection, not because you were once victimized, but because it is part of the human condition to be subject to harm and negative influences. A client of mine reasoned that leaving her sliding glass veranda door ajar in the hot summer evenings was safe enough because many of her neighbors did so. I asked her, "How does that make you safe?"

I have talked to people who think that if they can scream for help, they will be safe. In the meantime, they may be seriously hurt before help arrives (if it does). Are there times you reason in this way? What would you do to create safety?

Practice: The Shield Technique for Self-Protection

When you feel irritable or angry, is it because you feel you are getting the short end, being put upon, being taken for granted? (You may be thinking someone else is causing your trouble if you were abused in the past.)

Think of someone you believe is causing you to feel upset. Imagine a bright white shield between the two of you. Picture the other person on their side of the shield doing whatever behavior bothers you. As you picture their behavior and its negative energy moving toward the shield and you, let the shield absorb or block the negative energy. Fill up your side of the shield with images that are enjoyable or positive for you. This allows the other person to have their own energy while creating positive energy around you.

Practice: Diverting Arrows

If you have been told that you were wrong, stupid, that your parent wished you were never born, or other cruel things, you may have felt like a target at which others shot arrows. This could make you feel responsible, guilty, at fault, or to blame for everything that happens to you, as well as to others. You do not need to blame or fault others in order to protect yourself from these arrows. And you do not need to accept them. In the case of someone who abused you, you can learn to keep the arrow pointed away from you without losing the awareness that someone hurt you. (You need this awareness to protect yourself emotionally.)

Do this as an exercise with a particular person in mind. Imagine the person and what the arrow "says." Then turn the arrow away from you and register only the awareness that someone hurt you. This can allow you to be free of negative feeling toward others.

Practice: The Power in Confrontation

When you are confronting someone who has harmed or is harming you, if your measure of success is how they respond, you will feel hopeless and powerless. Create a realistic measure of success by setting goals you have the inner power to achieve.

For example: Goal: Letting someone know my discomfort with their drinking, smoking, etc. Objective: Suggest activities or times to spend with that person when the discomforting behavior will not be present.

A Closing Meditation: To the Underdog

Tears are "God's" pearls that help us wash away pain locked in the heart.

A Word (and Encouragement) to Dominators

If it has been important to you to be in control in your relationships, as a child you may have looked up to someone who seemed very powerful. Modeling yourself after this person offered you the illusion of control even if they misused their power over you (or others). Or perhaps as a child you were closely bonded to someone who seemed helpless and you felt you needed to take control. There could be many sources and explanations for your strivings. Western culture emphasizes control and power in many ways, from rewarding "take charge" behavior in men to expecting deference in women. But our purpose here is to offer you support in the knowledge that you can break out of this mental prison.

In your relationships, you can move all too easily from the one who controls, to bully, to victimizer. You are simply doing more of the same and sliding down the slippery slope to abusing. Some would say you already are abusing others. Abusing may be hurting others' feelings by putting them down, insulting, being impatient, controlling. Just thinking others are less than you can lead to demeaning behaviors on your part.

You may begin to realize that you have few friends or that there is a look of fear in others' eyes when you are speaking to them. This is not easy to acknowledge. But it is harder to live. On some level you already know something is wrong. But you can rise above the control these behaviors have on you. Your reward will be stepping out of the loneliness you are in and having connection with others.

The most important thing you can do is acknowledge what you already know. Once you see that your behaviors only alienate you from yourself and others, the trade-off won't seem so great. Your loss of power over others will generate reward in your life as well as within yourself.

Using This Book (For Those Who Skipped Ahead To This Section)

If you are picking up this book just to use this section, some explanations may help you. You may even want to read the entire book because, in every Dominator, there is the fear of being an Underdog. You may want to know what your partner has learned. If you use this information to continue dominating, you will lose either your Self, your partner, or both.

We do not presume that you are a man, abusing your partner, a woman. You may be a woman abusing a man. You may be a woman abusing another woman. Or you may be a man who is being abused but thinking you should be reading this section. Basically, this section is for anyone who is in an abusive relationship.

This book contains information about abuse, as well as meditations and personal exercises called "practices." The meditations are guided relaxations that include suggestions. If you want something of an emotional nature to "sink in," it will do so more readily if you are open or receptive. This is the opposite of how you may live your life generally. Proceed to the first meditation, written particularly for you, and refer back to it many times.

A Beginning Meditation: An Invitation to Inner Peace

Relax and prepare to take your mind off external concerns. Find a place where you can let down, somewhere no one will interrupt you or require you to be in control. Now relax further. You may use the Basic Meditation in Chapter Four if you choose to do so.

Search your mind for a memory of beauty. You may find this to be in nature, art, music. Once you have identified a memory of beauty, hold it in your mind. Focus on it alone. Let in the feelings you had when you first saw, felt or heard it...Extend this feeling in time for as long as you want to...Let in the feeling until you have learned it. Before you end, offer thanks.

Consider this meditation available to you when you need help controlling or changing your behavior.

Practice: Getting Off the Roller Coaster

If you have become accustomed to hurtful intensity in your relationships, it may be hard to believe that this is a problem. This is only because intensity is habit-forming; life might seem empty or boring without it. Learn to keep your joy-riding for work or play and make of your love life a more constant sharing.

Identify activities you can enjoy for intensity.

Practice: The Whole Is the Greatest

Fighting to stay on the top in your relationship is no different from persisting at staying on the bottom. If, on the other hand, you can allow a blending of part you and part your partner, something different from either of you can emerge. Then you have something greater than the sum of its parts. Are you ready to gain in your life? Consider it for the sake of your life.

Practice: Gaining by Losing

If you have been a Dominator type, it will be helpful for you to focus on gains you will achieve by relinquishing old behaviors. This will continue drawing you forward toward a much richer life.

Being a Dominator, for example, has brought you either competitive relationships, which keep you lonely, or follower-friends who are afraid to offer you their interests or honesty.

Take a look at your friendships. What kind of relationships are they?

Practice: Power Over/ Power Under

When you feel either above or below, better than or less than other people, you really are not connecting to them.

Remember some recent exchanges you had with people who are important to you in some way. What was the topic? What were you thinking about? Them? Yourself? The topic? Your plans for later? How to outsmart them? Some of these are examples of ways of avoiding contact. Which ones describe you? We all have occasional distractions or preoccupations, but how much avoiding do you do?

Practice: You Aren't Who You Appear to Be

Do you think domination is strength?

You may be thinking others do not see that you are in need of having power over them. You think that as long as you keep your position of domination, you control their knowledge of you. You may think that if they know you are trying to dominate them, they wouldn't allow it. If any of this is true, it probably would surprise you to know that most people see you for who you are. They either love you or put up with you in spite of yourself. But they do keep their distance from you.

How does it feel to know that others may be seeing your dominating behavior?

How does it feel to know that others may see how afraid you would be without it? Describe as many of your own dominating behaviors as you can—for example, acting "puffed up."

Practice: The Many Faces of Anger

We all feel a need for power in our lives. Somehow we must manage as we grow in age to grow in acceptance of what we can control and what we cannot. Do you get angry when you can't control or have your way? Do you get angry in order to intimidate others to get your way? Sometimes people will appease your anger and you get your way, but are you getting what you want in life? If you cannot yet accept the limits on your control, your very hard job is yet ahead. It's easy to intimidate others; much harder to grow in accepting not always being the one in control.

Make a list of some things you would like to be in control of.

Now list any of those things you may have to accept not having control of.

Practice: What Goes Around Comes Around

Unleashing anger or any strong negative emotion on your partner (or anyone else) damages you as well as them. As you create negativity in yourself, you invite it back. As you express it to others, you encourage its return to you.

Recall the last time you expressed anger toward someone. Review the situation and forget everything except how you felt inside yourself as you were angry. Tune in strongly. Note some words that describe this.

What do you want from others?

Practice: Ultimatums and Threats (Cutting Off Your Nose to Spite Your Face)

When you were five or six years old, did you ever try to run away from home? You were angry at one of your parents and thought you would get back at them for something. Do you remember that moment, perhaps a block or two from home, when you realized that not only could you not survive on your own, but no one had noticed your absence? It took all the energy out of your power struggle when you realized that you were alone. As an adult, you will be able to find others to fuel the energy of a power struggle. But are you any less lonely?

List some times when you were in power struggles that didn't get you anywhere.

Practice: Power Within

As you grow in your feeling of strength, competence, knowledge, or expertise, let this fill you inside with appreciation. Appreciation is a sense of power that is completely different from "power-over."

Imagine either learning a new skill or breaking your own record in a sport you enjoy. Concentrate on all the events surrounding this, whether it is something you create like a painting, or a new skill like archery, or swimming laps faster than ever. Turn this over in your mind, feel a sense of pride and satisfaction.

Describe one power-building activity you would like to do.

This is power.

Negotiating Your Relationship Forward

Negotiating is one of the most important skills to develop to move your relationship forward. If there are two people involved, you have differences. The trademark of a stuck relationship is the avoidance of dealing with these differences. Avoidance can exist in a variety of ways: one person may tune out their feelings of irritation and tune out their own needs. Another may yield because they feel they do not deserve their needs being addressed or they do not know how to negotiate. Some people use differences as an excuse to act out their needs, for example, in having affairs, gambling, or using drugs.

In previous chapters, you have worked on healing old wounds, valuing your feelings, understanding your needs, and on communicating to your partner. The following exercises are to help you learn the skill of negotiation. The hardest part is remembering to try it, and the next hardest is staying with it until you have resolution. There is *always* something to negotiate. You may need to yield to a basic need your partner has, but you can make up for that by having conditions placed on how the need is achieved. Likewise, you may need to stand your ground to meet a basic need of yours, but you may gain your partner's cooperation if you yield on the times or ways you meet your needs. The requirements of negotiation are that you and your partner are committed to changing your relationship and that you give and receive appreciation when you achieve resolution.

Phase One: Together as a team, choose one difference you wish to resolve. This should not be the most important issue either of you has. It should be a difference that periodically creates conflict or makes for unpleasantness but does not threaten the continuation of your relationship. (Save those for later.) You may need to negotiate a bit to choose where to start and, if it helps, you may designate a second difference for another time. Both of you should have paper and pen at hand.

Phase Two: Imagine your process as that of laying out your concerns on a table between you. Writing them or taking notes helps you focus on the problem rather than each other. Be careful not to elaborate too much on *why* something bothers you. You are at the negotiating table to make something work smoothly, not to develop personal insight or start a quarrel. If at a later time you wish to learn more about each other with such sharing, that's always okay. But first learn how to accommodate your different sets of needs. This is a respect-building process that can carry over in deeper discussions later.

Phase Two is your opportunity to state what bothers you about the difference between you. An example may be that partner #1 has an interest, a hobby, or friendship she wishes to spend time on, and partner #2 resents either time spent away, money spent, or being left out. Perhaps the solution has seemed to partner #2 that partner #1 entirely give up the diversion.

Phase Three: Phase Three is the time to discuss how partner #1 can meet that need in a way that meets some of partner #2's needs. This phase involves compromise. Partner #1 may give up some of the times or ways to do the activity in question and partner #2 may give up the demand that the activity stop altogether.

Phase Three may take days to discuss. Each party may make proposals or suggestions and require time to elapse to consider his or her feelings. This phase should *not* be hurried. Not only will speed lend itself to creating more conflict, but it will block the partners' individual processes in determining an agreement they can live with.

Phase Four: Phase Four is the time when an initial agreement becomes formalized. The partners should write down their agreements and conditions. The situation that would previously have caused conflict is presented along with the new plan of action. The new time or way partner #1 is going to proceed is specified, and the ways that this will better meet partner #2's needs is also stated. If both partners feel comfortable with the plan, continue with the next phase.

Phase Five: Proceed to setting up the next occasion of the debated activity. Both partners can fine tune their needs as the reality is dealt with.

Phase Six: This is the time to express to each other a job well done and appreciation you each hold for the other's participation in working it out.

Practice: Growing Cooperative

You are not enemies. Your enemies are within: emptiness, your personal history, fear. The more you can be in the present with yourself and your partner, the less your past hurt will affect you. Imagine yourselves as a circus high-wire act or a mountain-climbing team. Would you be saying, "I'm not going to catch you this time because of the last time you missed me?"

Consider that in every moment you are in contact, you are choosing to be an adversary or a team player. Discuss this image together. If you choose to put this concept into practice, be patient since you could take weeks to create this cooperative foreground for your relationship. If ever you are inclined to blame or point out to your partner that he or she is failing, tell yourself you are going to pass on that. Refocus on your own learning process and remember with compassion how much work you are doing. Remember also that each time you fail is an opportunity to learn.

Practice: Primacy or Possessiveness?

Having a partner who is Number One in your life requires mutual trust that neither of you will abuse this honor. Abuse in this case would mean trying to control, thinking you know what's best for the other, presuming he or she is with you to meet your needs.

When you become aware of being possessive, make a note of how this feels.

tight . . . . *.loose*

tense . . . . *.relaxed*

greedy . . . . *.generous*

closed . . . . *.open*

Switch roles. Can you imagine your partner deciding whether you prefer blue or red? Dancing or biking? Fish or rice? Math or art? What makes your relationship strong is if you appreciate your differences as well as your similarities. Your team can walk forward only if you have both a right and a left leg.

Practice: Benefit-of-the-Doubt Kindness

Besides teamwork and primacy, your relationship requires benefit-of-the-doubt kindness. You may know this as: "Give the guy a break;" "Just let it go;" or "Hey, everyone has their problems." It's that time when you want to strike out because your partner has been irritable with you or you may be feeling rejected because your partner can't pay attention to you. These are times to let him or her "off the hook."

In this gesture, you are giving benefit-of-the-doubt kindness. Once you realize your partner's mood or action has little to do with you, you may be ready to feel compassion. When we are having a bad day, a supportive partner can be the greatest gift we may receive.

Cool-Downs, Diversions, and Dating

Cool-Downs (and Time-Outs)

We have referred to the need to control your anger and your behavior. Here we offer some different approaches and exercises so you can find a combination for cooling down that works for you. If you are becoming angry, start by telling your partner that you are taking a time-out and stating a time period. Generally, for a cool-down time, you will need to physically separate, even if it is just to another room. Discuss this ahead of time with your partner. Always use a time-out to be distracted. This allows you to dilute your anger with some reality.

A Mini-Meditation *(See "The Eight-Count Exercise" in Chapter 4)*

Sit by yourself. Close your eyes. Take a long, deep breath and, breathing through your nose, slowly inhale to the count of four, exhale to the count of eight. (You may choose other numbers but the exhale should be double the inhale number.) Do this at least ten times.

Go to Your Favorite Place

Sit by yourself. Close your eyes. Imagine you are in your favorite kind of place: by the ocean, in the mountains, in an open field, next to a secluded stream. Relax and settle in. Notice the things around you that you like. It may be the sound of waves, the feel of sand under your feet, the roll of the mountain tops, the ripple or glimmer of running water, the soft cushion of grass beneath you. It may be the warmth of sun or the coolness of shade. Absorb all the feelings and sensations, the sights and sounds that you like. Allow lots of time and stay until you feel relaxed and refreshed. (Practice this when you are not stressed so that when you need it, you can do it.)

Exercise

If you are a runner, walker, or biker, you have an outlet that is easily accessible. Just be sure you don't use this as an avoidance of conflict. Cool-downs are only to relieve the tension that caused abusive behavior, loss of control, or temper outburst.

Music

Listen to or play relaxing or expansive music only. If you like fast-paced music, choose this only if it helps your anger to dissipate.

Use cool-downs as a genuine opportunity to relax. Do not go over and over what made you mad. And do not use it to test your partner and return saying, "See, I'm still mad." This is a chance to take responsibility for the way *you* deal with *your* feelings.

Diversions (and Taking a Break)

You need rejuvenation just like your relationship does. If you get it, you will automatically help bring energy and vitality to your relationship. If you resent your partner's autonomy, work on Chapters Four, Five, and Six. Other good resources to consult about dealing with your control or dependency needs are Melody Beattie's early books on "co-dependency."

If you already pursue hobbies, friendships, and activities on your own, you probably need to focus more on connecting with your partner. If your focus has been constant on your partner, you need to begin taking steps to develop more autonomy.

In this section we will propose different exercises based on whether you are a man or woman. The exercises themselves will indicate how different our gender training is.

For Women (Mostly)

The Restaurant Exercise

If you have seldom or never done so, take yourself out to a restaurant alone. Begin by going for tea or coffee, mid-morning or mid-afternoon. Build up to taking yourself out alone for dinner. You can use aids like the newspaper or a book at the beginning, but be sure to take some time with just you and your meal.

Finding Yourself/Finding Time

Sign up for a class to learn a hobby, or begin an activity you have been wanting to do. Find a way to get the time. If you facilitate free time for your partner (for example, if you have children or run a business together), see that free time is also arranged for you.

Learning With Others

Read A Room of One's Own *by Virginia Woolf, or a collection of Doris Lessing's short stories. Join or set up a discussion group with other women to read about women's lives.*

For Men (Mostly)

The Restaurant Exercise

If you usually spend off-work time alone or with your partner, make a date for lunch with a male friend or co-worker. Do this enough so that it becomes an easy habit.

Finding Yourself/Finding Time

If you are used to filling your time with activities, hobbies, sports, or television, take some of this time to be quiet and by yourself. Watch a campfire, take a slow stroll, read a book, start a diary of reflections on your life, your needs, your changing.

Learning With Others

You may normally try to learn new things by yourself. Some men have an aversion to asking questions. If you are one of these, take a class where you will have an instructor to learn from. Practice asking questions.

Dating (and Coming Together)

If you have learned to control your temper, know when you need to be separate or quiet, and know how to follow your own interests. The most important thing you can bring into your life and your partnership is the act of dating. If you have continued this and your relationship is in trouble, you may want to look back again at the dynamics between you. If you "go out" and all that happens is bickering, you need to go back to earlier steps.

Practice: Dating Your Partner

Remember when you were first getting to know your partner. You were curious. You may have discussed common interests. You exchanged information about yourselves and found out how you were alike and how you were different, what you liked and what you didn't like. Basically, you were interested in the other person. (If you weren't, you get to develop that now.) If your relationship is already established you may have forgotten how to be interested in your partner. Dating is time to enjoy an activity together and time to keep knowing each other.

Make a list of things you might want to know about or discuss with your partner. (Remember how you would talk to a friend: "How are things going for you now?")

If you try this exercise and you are bored, it's because you need to listen more closely and ask more questions.

Practice: Enjoy

Your sexual relationship is an opportunity to express love, tenderness, and kindness. It should be a gift and, in the giving, you receive gratification.

To learn this, practice exchanges with your partner. Take turns, for perhaps fifteen minutes each, giving some form of non-sexual touch your partner likes. This may be any combination of soft touch, back-scratching, a body or foot massage, etc. Tune into what your partner wants and the doing of it. Look for your enjoyment in giving pleasure. You will be able to transfer this to your sexual relationship.

Practice: Time to Date Someone New?

If you get overly absorbed in wanting to be close to someone new, this is the time to practice restraint, patience, and to *refocus.* If you have had abusive relationships or have had trouble staying with one primary relationship, changing these patterns is what you are needing to do if you are working with this book. You may be wanting to get away from your primary relationship because it is hard work. New flirtations are *always* easier than making a long-term partnership healthy. If you have the urge, though, there are a number of things you can do. First of all, take it easy on yourself. Don't beat yourself up for having thoughts. Use it instead as a signal that you need to work with yourself. If you are overwhelmed in your life or by the demands of your relationship, a flirtation may be the signal to direct you to better self-care. You may need a break; you probably need help dealing with your feelings; you need some time. These are things you may need to negotiate for with your partner.

Have you had this need for a flirtation in the past? Now that you know yourself better, what did it mean? If you acted on your feelings and had an affair, how did it work out? What happened to your partnership during that time? Putting feelings aside, do you think it would be a good idea? Have you discussed it with your partner?

Practice: Flirtation—A New One or Anew

A New Flirtation

Try on your fantasy. Go all the way with it. Indulge it. Draw it out. Where do you want it to go?

Is this realistic?

How does this meet your current goals?

Flirting Anew

Flirting is a way you get to be in touch with a light-hearted, attractive, attracting part of yourself. What do you like about yourself when you flirt?

Try flirting with your partner. How does he or she respond?

Flirting anew can renew your partnership and be fun.

Closing Words of Encouragement: Depth Markers

In our culture of acquisition and competition, "more" and "new" are valued; duration and depth are elusive in many ways, including in relationships. If you and your partner are working to create a healthier, more egalitarian relationship, you are already deepening. Don't expect to feel this constantly, but when you do, embrace the feeling and acknowledge to yourself and your partner that you have felt it. This is like a marker on a running or biking trail: it fills you with enough confidence and positive energy to continue on your venture.

The Scene of Healthy Relationships: Heart to Heart

In setting the scene for how you want your relationship to look, act, and feel, the idea that you are a unit and on the same team will be very different from the battling of competitors that you may have gotten used to. If you are a team and you attack the other person, you are depleting and diminishing *yourself*. If you have grown accustomed to having to fight to be heard or having to be hurt whenever you stand up for yourself, hopefully you have begun to reorient yourself and are now separating yourself out from these old beliefs.

You and your partner will move at different speeds with these concepts, and each of you should discuss your feelings about these changes of belief. If your value systems are congruent, you may find that you can help each other remember the new concepts. You may need to go over and over this new idea of being a unit, of being two parts of a whole. This change is so radical for some of us raised in our culture of competition that it may be the most difficult change to make.

We have talked about dealing with feelings and learning about who you are and who you want to become. The following thoughts are for you to consider as you move into fuller relationships with others. One of our blessings can be the joy that comes from sharing the human experience with others who are having it and growing in it, too.

Exercise: Heart to Heart (Do with Your Partner)

Stand in a relaxed posture facing each other and breathe easily. Close your eyes. Be aware of your own body. Imagine moving a stream of light from the top of your head down to your abdomen. Go slowly and feel these areas open to the light.

Now focus on warmth and light in your chest. If you can enjoy this openness, you are ready to embrace your partner into it. With the warmth filling you, think of or look at your partner. Let your heart embrace your partner.

You should do this exercise so often that you can identify it happening or make it happen at least once a day. You can work at this like working a new muscle, and become so adept that even when you are differing with your partner, you can create this feeling. You are now capable of creating a heart-to-heart connection that will serve you and your relationship for as long as you choose.

Closing Contemplation (Food for Thought)

Blending Anger into the Fold

When you feel disconnected or angry with your partner, go to your safe place, imagine the beauty, the color, the calm, the sounds. Let these positive feelings radiate inside you. Then turn to your partner and extend these feelings outward. Words may be unnecessary.

Spiritual Authority

Trust your spiritual self above all others. This will give you a healthy perspective on the purpose and limits of all your relationships. With those you choose to trust intimately, always know that you and your spiritual self are the only experts on you.

The Flow of To and Fro

Your relationship is like the blowing of sea grass on a beautiful beach. You have the opportunity for a master dance if you can bend and yield, approach and draw inward, excite and allow.

Afterword: Life with Gentleness

You would not be reading these pages if you were not taking up the challenge of healing and changing. Life is process; so is healing. There is no finished product, no end to it. Some of us hope we can be "finished," which is a way to close the door to that room which contains pain. We could forget our hurts and we could be free of pain. This book is about the choice to open doors in order to open to healing. Otherwise we remain wounded behind closed doors. Our feelings and behaviors get tied up in knots with nowhere to go. We wind and unwind, rewind and unwind, until our existence is a well-worn path of unhappiness.

To attain closure is different from being closed, however. When we reach closure, it means we are able to manage our lives in positive ways, ways that foster warmth in ourselves and mutuality and warmth in our relationships. Closure means that our rooms have doors but they all have well-oiled hinges. We have the ability and facility to open and close all parts of ourselves with warmth and compassion.

This book has been about opening the door of unhappiness and victimization and spreading warmth and compassion throughout that room so that whenever there is a knock on that door, a spur to our memory, a need to protect, we can move gracefully into that room because we carry love in our footsteps. We can seek out the feelings or memories that need comfort, give nurturance, and gently leave the room once again like we quietly leave the room of a sleeping child.

Let the sleeping child be guarded and loved. There is always the morning of awakening to what lies ahead as the journey continues. Because the journey lasts as long as we do, we must remember to create joy and relaxation and love along the path.

SUGGESTED READINGS

Inspiration

Muller, Wayne, M.Div. *Legacy of the Heart*. Fireside, 1993.
Peck, M. Scott, M.D. *The Road Less Traveled*. New York: Simon & Schuster, 1998.
Peck, M. Scott, M.D. *People of the Lie*. New York: Simon & Schuster, 1997.

On Dealing with Depression

Burns, David. *Feeling Good: The New Mood Therapy*. Avon, 1992.

On Healing

Achterberg, Jeanne, Ph.D., Barbara Dassey, RN, MS, Leslie Kolkmeier, RN, M.Ed. *Rituals of Healing: Using Imagery for Health and Wellness*. Bantam Doubleday Dell, 1994.

Beattie, Melody. *Codependent No More*. San Francisco: Harper/Hazelden, 1986.

Dolan, Yvonne, MH. *One Small Step: Moving Beyond Trauma and Therapy to a Life of Joy*. Papier Mache Press, 1998.

Gawain, Shakti. *Creative Visualization*. New World Library, 1995.

Gawain, Shakti. *Living in the Light: A Guide to Personal and Planetary Transformation*. New World Library, 1998.

Hanh, Thich Nhat. *Being Peace*. Parallax Press, 1988.

On Meditation

Hanh, Thich Nhat. *The Miracle of Mindfulness: A Manual on Meditation*. Boston: Beacon Press, 1992.

Levine, Stephen. *A Gradual Awakening*. Anchor, 1989.

On Recovering from Trauma

Bass, Ellen and Laura Davis. *The Courage to Heal*. New York: Harper and Row, 1989.

Carnes, Patrick J., Ph.D. *The Betrayal Bond.* Health Communications Inc., 1997.

Engel, Beverly, MFCC. *The Emotionally Abused Woman: Overcoming Destructive Patterns and Reclaiming Yourself.* New York: Fawcett Books, 1992.

Evans, Patricia. *The Verbally Abusive Relationship: How to Recognize It and How to Respond.* Adams Publications, 1996.

Herman, Judith. *Trauma and Recovery: The Aftermath of Violence.* New York: Basic Books, 1993.

Martin, Del. *Battered Wives.* San Francisco: Volcano Press, 1989.

Matsakis, Aphrodite, Ph.D. *Trust After Trauma: A Guide to Relationships for Survivors and Those Who Love Them.* Oakland: New Harbinger Publications, 1998.

NiCarthy, Ginny, MSW. *Getting Free: You Can End Abuse and Take Back Your Life.* Seal Press, 1997.

Walker, Lenore. *Battered Woman.* New York: Harper Collins, 1980.

Wilson, K.J., Ed.D. *When Violence Begins at Home: A Comprehensive Guide to Understanding and Ending Domestic Abuse.* Hunter House, 1997. (A combined project of the Austin Center for Battered Women and the National Domestic Violence Hotline)

Working with Men Who Abuse

Lindsey, Michael, Robert McBride, and Constance M. Platt. *Philosophy and Curriculum for Treating Batterers.* Littleton, Co.: Gylantic Publishing Co., 1993.

Pence, Ellen, and Michael Paymar. *Education Groups for Men Who Batter: The Duluth Model.* New York: Springer Publishing Co., 1993.

THE AUTHOR

Carolyn McGinnis received her Ph.D. in psychology from The Wright Institute in 1982. She supervised counseling programs at the University of Minnesota and California College of Arts and Crafts and served as the co-chair of Minnesota Women Psychologists. Dr. McGinnis has specialized as a supervisor and psychotherapist to women and couples in a variety of clinical settings for over 26 years while maintaining private practices in Berkeley, California, and Minneapolis, Minnesota. She speaks to professional and public audiences on psychiatric diagnoses and interpersonal dynamics.

In recent years, Dr. McGinnis has applied a transpersonal perspective to her work with clients having post-traumatic stress disorder, as well as couples in destructive relationships. Her spiritual studies and writing have taken her to Santa Fe, New Mexico, where she is the Intake Coordinator for that city's Community Guidance Center. This is Dr. McGinnis' first book; a second book is in progress.

Life is an ongoing journey of change and evolution in all realms of existence. Our mission at Heartsfire is to help you understand life's process and to provide books that offer guidance in the search for truth, self, and clarity. We are privileged to present original and compelling writers who speak from their hearts and guide us to the magic of everyday experience. If you have a manuscript that you feel is suitable for us, we would love to hear from you. Send a letter of inquiry to: *Acquisitions Editor*, **Heartsfire Books**, 500 N. Guadalupe Street, Suite G-465, Santa Fe, New Mexico 87501 USA. Email: heartsfirebooks@heartsfirebooks.com. Visit us at http://www.heartsfirebooks.com.

Heartsfire Consciousness Literature

Creating an Abuse-Free Relationship:
A Manual for Recovering Self and Intimacy
Carolyn McGinnis
March 1999

Sacred Life, Holy Death:
Seven Stages of Crossing the Divide
Robert Boldman
April 1999

The Alchemy of Love:
A Pilgrimage of Sacred Discovery
Robert Boldman

The Emerald Covenant:
Spiritual Rites of Passage
Michael E. Morgan

Fathers:
Transforming Your Relationship
John Selby

Gifts from Spirit:
A Skeptic's Path
Dennis Augustine

Healing Depression:
A Guide to Making Intelligent Choices about Treating Depression
Catherine Carrigan

Health for Life:
Secrets of Tibetan Ayurveda
Robert Sachs
Foreword by Dr. Lobsang Rapgay

Hermanos de la Luz:
Brothers of the Light
Ray John de Aragón

Inescapable Journey:
A Spiritual Adventure
Claude Saks

In the Presence of My Enemies:
Memoirs of Tibetan Nobleman Tsipon Shuguba
Sumner Carnahan with Lama Kunga Rinpoche

Message from the Sparrows:
Engaging Consciousness
Taylor Morris

The Search for David:
A Cosmic Journey of Love
George Schwimmer

Solitude:
The Art of Living with Yourself
John Selby

Spirtuality for the Business Person:
Inner Practices for Success
Claude Saks

Strong Brew:
One Man's Prelude to Change
Claude Saks

Tibet:
Enduring Spirit, Exploited Land
Robert Z. Apte and Andrés R. Edwards
Foreword and Poem by His Holiness the Dalai